T0084743

Aquinas on Crime

Other Titles of Interest from St. Augustine's Press

Plato, *The Symposium of Plato: The Shelley Translation*. Translated by Percy Bysshe Shelley.

Aristotle, *Aristotle – On Poetics*. Translated by Seth Benardete and Michael Davis

Aristotle, *Physics, Or Natural Hearing*. Translated by Glen Coughlin.

St. Augustine, *On Order [De Ordine]*. Translated by Silvano Borruso.

St. Augustine, *The St. Augustine LifeGuide: Words to Live by from the Great Christian Saint*. Translated by Silvano Borruso,

Michael Davis, *The Poetry of Philosophy*

Thomas Aquinas, *Commentary on Aristotle's Nicomachean Ethics*

Thomas Aquinas, *Commentary on Aristotle's De Anima*

Thomas Aquinas, *Commentary on Aristotle's Metaphysics*

Thomas Aquinas, *Commentary on Aristotle's Posterior Analytics*

Thomas Aquinas, *Commentary on Aristotle's Physics*

Thomas Aquinas, *Disputed Questions on Virtue*. Translated by Ralph McInerny

Thomas Aquinas, *Commentary on the Epistle to the Hebrews*. Translated by Chrysostom Baer, O. Praem.

Thomas Aquinas, *Commentaries on St. Paul's Epistles to Timothy, Titus, and Philemon*. Translated by Chrysostom Baer, O. Praem.

John of St. Thomas, *Introduction to the Summa Theologiae of Thomas Aquinas*. Translated by Ralph McInerny.

John Poinsot [John of St. Thomas], *Tractatus de Signis Poinsot: The Semiotic of John Poinsot*.

Seth Benardete, *Sacred Transgressions: A Reading of Sophocles' Antigone*

Seth Benardete, *Herodoean Inquiries*

Josef Pieper, *Leisure, the Basis of Culture*

Josef Pieper, *Scholasticism: Personalities and Problems*

Josef Pieper, *The Silence of St. Thomas*

Francisco Suarez, *On Creation, Conservation, & Concurrence: Metaphysical Disputations 20–22*. Translated by A.J. Freddoso

Francisco Suarez, *Metaphysical Demonstration of the Existence of God*. Translated by John P. Doyle

Jacques Maritain, *Natural Law: Reflections on Theory and Practice*

Henrik Syse, *Natural Law, Religion, and Rights*

Fulvio di Blasi, *God and the Natural Law: A Rereading of Thomas Aquinas*

Joseph Bobik, *Veritas Divina: Aquinas on Divine Truth*

Joseph Owens, C.Ss.R., *Aristotle's Gradations of Being in Metaphysics E–Z*

Aquinas on Crime

Charles P. Nemeth

ST. AUGUSTINE'S PRESS
South Bend, Indiana

Copyright © 2008 by Charles P. Nemeth

All rights reserved. No part of this book may be reproduced, stored in a retrieval system, or transmitted, in any form or by any means, electronic, mechanical, photocopying, recording, or otherwise, without the prior permission of St. Augustine's Press.

Manufactured in the United States of America.

1 2 3 4 5 6 14 13 12 11 10 09 08

Library of Congress Cataloging in Publication Data
Nemeth, Charles P., 1951–
    Aquinas on crime / Charles P. Nemeth.
        p. cm.
    Includes index.
    ISBN-13: 978-1-58731-030-0 (hardcover: alk. paper)
    ISBN-10: 1-58731-030-9 (hardcover: alk. paper
    ISBN-13: 978-1-58731-031-7 (paperbound: alk. paper
    ISBN-10: 1-58731-031-7 (paperbound: alk. paper)
    1. Thomas, Aquinas, Saint, 1225?–1274. 2. Criminal law. I. Title.
    K447.T4N465 2007
    345 – dc22   2007028842

∞ The paper used in this publication meets the minimum requirements of the American National Standard for Information Sciences – Permanence of Paper for Printed Materials, ANSI Z39.48-1984.

ST AUGUSTINE'S PRESS
www.staugustine.net

To: Ralph Masiello, Michael Strasser, and Roland Ramirez – dedicated scholars in the world of St. Thomas.

To: St. Thomas Aquinas who stated: "There are, however, some virtues, whose acts must endure throughout the whole of life, such as faith, hope and charity, since they regard the last end of the entire life of men." – *Summa Theologica* II-II Question 137, art 1

Contents

Contents

Acknowledgments

As in all text projects, the author has come to depend upon a circle of generous figures. First, I was blessed to have an excellent Graduate Assistant in Adam Young, whose research skills really helped in a significant sense. At the editorial phase of putting the book together, I appreciate the skill and assistance of Hope Haywood. Those who run our offices at CAL U, namely Laurie Manderino and Rose Mahouski, surely provide an environment for the writer to write – a condition I am forever thankful for. At California University of Pennsylvania I am most fortunate to have superiors who value the role of scholarship in the university. President Angelo Armenti, Provost Sean Madden, and Dean Len Colelli are model administrators and scholars in their own right.

At St. Augustine's Press it was nothing but easy working with Bruce Fingerhut. I am impressed with both the editorial and production side of this fine press.

In my own house, my partner of 36 years, Jean Marie, and the seven wonderful children God has loaned to me, drive many enterprises including this text. Eleanor, Stephen, Anne Marie, John, Joseph, Mary Claire, and Michael Augustine cause unceasing joy in my life.

And finally, to the many Thomists have encountered in my lifetime, I owe a deep debt of gratitude. I dedicate this text to three of the best Thomists I have ever encountered – Ralph Masiello, Michael Strasser, and Roland Ramirez. It is often said that Professors sometimes do not discern the differences they make in people's lives. These three scholars should be assured that their presence in the classroom has significantly impacted a host of people.

Preface

NOT MUCH ESCAPES THE INTELLECT AND IMAGINATION OF THE ANGELIC Doctor, St. Thomas Aquinas. Few contemporaries realize how Aquinas was and still is on the cutting edge of most things. Whether it be love, children, education, moral reasoning, happiness or the proper dispositions for human existence, St. Thomas seems an expert in all of it. I am forever amazed by his substance, but sometimes even more impressed by his prophetic and insightful mind- a man well before his time on just about every topic. Crime and criminal conduct is no exception to this general tendency with him. Not only does he have much to say about it, but what he relates is perpetually fresh and surely the bedrock of what many of us now take for granted. In a word, his intellect makes the rest of us feel very small and especially humble.

In this short treatise, the focus targets St. Thomas' criminal codification. Indeed the magnanimity of his crimes code is a subject matter not yet treated in any detail in the scholarly literature. While parts and pieces are covered in many quarters, the literature has yet to develop a systematic, codified examination of Thomistic criminal law. This probably arises for several reasons. First, few legal practitioners have either the time or the inclination to examine the esoteric subject matter. To be sure, most practitioners, let alone philosophical types, are not familiar with the depth and breadth of his criminal coverage. Second, the philosophical generally avoids, or might be unfamiliar with, something that is exclusively the province of a crimes code. Third, few authors are comfortable blending the two worlds of discovery, namely legal practice and Thomism. After nearly three decades of legal practice, much of which has been bound up in the theory and analysis of criminal law, I am ready to craft, however imperfectly, this piece on the

Thomist Criminal Code. My other occupation as "philosopher," though admittedly a novice and amateur when compared to the likes of Aquinas, fosters the project.

The essence of the endeavor is threefold: first, how does St. Thomas factor the nature of the human person into the concept of criminal culpability and personal responsibility; second, what types of criminal conduct does St. Thomas specifically delineate and define; and lastly, what is Thomas' view of mitigation and defense, as well as the corresponding punishment meted out for criminal conduct? This short commentary zeroes in on Thomistic Criminal Law – a project which will illuminate the root, the heritage and the foundation of modern criminal codification. As usual, St. Thomas arrived at the station long before the train ever left the gate.

Chapter 1
Aquinas and the Idea of Law

Introduction

BEFORE EXAMINING THE CRIMINAL LAW THEORY OF ST. THOMAS, IT IS critical to understand his perception and understanding of law. For the modern practitioner, law will be wrapped up in strict promulgation and codification. The very power of law will be in its enactment. This is true of any sort of law, whether it be criminal or civil, administrative or maritime. Law, in brief, consists of the words that emerge from the legislative process. Rape, murder, or theft finds meaning and definition in the definition of the law itself. Positivism, which holds that laws derive their force and power from promulgation, is the predominant jurisprudence.

This approach is woefully inadequate in the world of St. Thomas. In contrast, his vision is properly described as "eudaemonistic and teleological" and "Natural."[1] Criminal law, like any other category of human law is "designed to help men lead the best possible lives."[2] Law may take the form of enactment or code, and come into existence by promulgation and other legislative process, but this characterization dwells upon a singular facet of Thomas' jurisprudence. To exclusively depend on the promulgations of man, St. Thomas holds, erects a jurisprudence of futility. J.V. Dolan contends: "Legal positivism. . . . as a formulated theory of law . . . is fighting a losing battle."[3]

Aquinas respects promulgation, but only to a point. For Aquinas gazes at higher orders – the natural, the divine and the eternal. When human laws are inconsistent with these higher orders he will even encourage civil disobedience to the promulgation and even deny said promulgation has the force or effect of "law.." Unjust laws do not bind in conscience, says St. Thomas.

> On the other hand, laws may be unjust in two ways: first, by
> being contrary to the human good, through being opposed
> to the things mentioned above- either in respect to the end
> . . . or in respect of the author, as when a man makes a law
> that goes beyond the power committed to him . . .[4]

Hence when laws are contrary to or inconsistent with to the natural law or the eternal law of God, these are "acts of violence rather than laws." Such laws "do not bind in conscience."[5] According to Aquinas, unjust laws are not laws at all.[6] For Thomas, there is a "law that is beyond the law" which guides human operations. Igor Grazin labels this law the "Imperatives of the Highest Nature" given "us by the mercy and wisdom of the truly Supreme Legislator."[7] This law, consisting of first principles, secondary deductions, and prudential insights – impressions of the Creator that shape our essence, which is burned and impressed into our very fiber – is just as much part of our humanity and legal infra-structure as the codification. Noel McDermott remarks:

> There is a sense in which the law is inhuman, but the law
> beyond the law is entirely human, and the judge who takes
> account of it is simply thinking in human terms as well as
> legal terms. . . . The law beyond the law is simply the law of
> his own humanness, an intuition of the human in himself
> which demands great lucidity and humility.[8]

All law, criminal or otherwise, maintains its connection to this law above the law and "retain[s] a certain universality" and "impose[s] some rational pattern on an otherwise chaotic element" known as the collective.[9] Crimes and the criminal law that defines behavior means much more than the terms and descriptions of proscription. The crimes code, which police, prosecutors, and judges so slavishly interpret, is the tip of the legal iceberg. The need for criminal laws simply reflects human frailty and errors. Criminals fail to "grasp basic features of human well-being" and suffer from "deformities of conscience due to deprived social or moral histories" and from "defects of reasoning."[10] Compellingly, St. Thomas argues that human beings need law as a form of habituation and training, and without the regularizing influences, the bulk of the populace would descend into the strictly pleasurable. In his *Commentary on Aristotle's Nicomachean Ethics*, he poses this extraordinary ideal for a law:

> But it is difficult, he shows that legislation is required for virtuous habituation. First, he shows that all men become virtuous by means of law. Next . . . he shows that this cannot be done properly without law. . . . And that it is difficult for anyone to be guided from his youth to virtue according to good customs unless he is reared under excellent laws by which a kind of necessity impels a man to good.[11]

In this sense, law is necessary for the masses on two fronts: first, for the already good to give support and sustenance to their goodness, and secondly, to those who operate only out of consequence or fear.

In order to understand law, criminal or otherwise, one needs to understand man. When engaged in criminal activity, men make conscious choices about objectives and ends. Criminals, through flawed choices, are "diverted from human fulfillment."[12] Any real hope at understanding the criminal theory of St. Thomas will largely depend on the mastery of his psychology.[13] To appreciate St. Thomas, the reader must review the fundamentals of his jurisprudence and ask the most rudimentary question – What is law?

The Thomistic Idea of Law

When contemporary thinkers employ the term "law," they yearn for definition – an anchor, a foundation of meaning. Exactly what a law means depends on perspective. A common conception of law is that of a rule, regulation, statute, or ordinance, a case issued by judicial authority, or some other concretization of a particular legal idea or principle. *Laws* are as numerous and meaningful as the scope of their coverage, and are, without much argument, *juridical* instruments. By *juridical* the law's content commands, prohibits, enhances, advances, or restricts a good or end. As comprehended by St. Thomas, law is juridical,[14] but only partially. Thomas paints the broadest picture of law possible. First, law is synonymous with God, with rationality, and a rational plan of creation and operations. Even the irrational creature, as directed by God through natural inclination, has a legalistic quality. Law pertains to the species. Modern-day legal thinkers would be confused by the comprehensiveness of his definition:

> Just as the acts of irrational creatures are directed by God through a rational plan which pertains to their species, so

are the acts of men directed by God inasmuch as they pertain to the individual, as we have shown. But the acts of irrational creatures, as pertaining to the species, are directed by God through natural inclination, which goes along with the nature of the species. Therefore, over and above this, something must be given to men whereby they may be directed in their own personal acts. And this we call law.[15]

Therefore, Thomistic law defines itself in a more profound sense beyond promulgation, for the law's essence mirrors the fullness of God's creation, the nature of his creatures, and the unfolding of species and their corresponding operations. Law is supreme, divine legislation in addition to its positive codification or ordinance; it is the plan for a life consistent with this divine rationality – a life of virtue, and it is the order "whereby man clings to God."[16]

Law as the "Rule and Measure" of Reason

In Thomas' view, law is a "certain rational plan and rule of operation"[17] and especially proper "to rational creatures only."[18] St. Thomas confidently asserts that "law is something pertaining to reason"[19] and a measure of human activity (*Ergo lex est aliquid rationis*). If it is a measure of human action, one must presuppose there is a connection to human reason, since only the human species analyzes, deliberates, and counsels about activity and movement. St. Thomas asserts that law is a rational exercise:

> Since law is a kind of rule and measure, it may be in something in two ways. First, as in that which measures and rules and since this is proper to reason, it follows that, in this way, law is in the reason alone. Secondly, as in that which is ruled and measured. In this way, law is in all those things that are inclined to something by reason of some law, so that any inclination arising from a law may be called a law.[20]

Law is entwined with being itself. Some have argued that St. Thomas' perspective on law is almost cosmic – a reflection of how all movement occurs, whether that of the heavenly body, the animal or plant, or the laws of physics. Anton-Hermann Chroust discovers a *universal cosmic orderliness* in Thomistic jurisprudence:

> First, the ontological order in which being as such tends towards the preservation of its own being in accordance

with its ontological nature. In the case of man this inclination manifests itself in the preservation of life and in all of man's actions conducive to this preservation. Secondly, the vitalistic order in which being tends towards positive action. In the case of man this tendency becomes an inclination to act appropriately and in accordance with his own being and purpose. And, thirdly, the order of the rational and social animal which is also the domain of free moral self-determination.[21]

In a way, each of Chroust's assertions is valid because St. Thomas perceives law as an ordination, an impetus, an activity seeking proper ends, a fulfillment of essence and perfection of operation. Etienne Gilson eloquently corroborates:

> The first, and the most vast of all, is the universe. All beings created by God and maintained in existence by His will, can be regarded as one huge society in which all of us are members, along with animals, and even with things. There is not a single creature, animate or inanimate, which does not act in conformity with certain ends. Animals and things are subject to these rules and tend toward their ends without knowing them. Man, on the contrary, is conscious of them, and his moral justice consists in accepting them voluntarily. All the laws of nature, all the laws of morality or of society ought to be considered as so many particular cases of one single law, divine law. Now, God's rule for the government of the universe is, like God Himself, necessarily eternal. Thus the name *eternal law* is given to this first law, sole source of all others.[22]

Stated concisely, the law represents rationality and orderliness in individual and rational existence. Law, aside from its enactment, is the handmaiden of reason itself. When dealing with the law's essence, St. Thomas imparts primary stature to reason:

> Law is a rule and measure of acts, whereby man is induced to act or is restrained from acting; for *lex* [*law*] is derived from *ligare* [*to bind*], because it binds one to act. Now the rule and measure of human acts is the reason, which is the first principle of human acts, as is evident from what has been stated above. For it belongs to the reason to direct to the end, which is the first principle in all matters of action, according to the Philosopher.[23]

Law as an Instrument of the Common Good

Since man is a social animal, any legitimate theory of law extends to a culture, a community, a civilization. St. Thomas is well aware that the ordinating influence of law does not terminate with individual activity, because it just as pertinently applies to the common good of a nation as it applies to the common good of its individual citizenry. In response to whether a law should be crafted for the individual or common case, St. Thomas indicates that every human law derives legitimacy from its relationship to the common interest. Laws consist of far more than individual applications but are germane to the life of a nation. "Hence human laws should be proportioned to the common good. Now the common good comprises many things. Therefore law should take account of many things, as to persons, as to matters, and as to times."[24]

With keen insight, Thomas discerns the futility of a law that applies in the individual scenario alone. Laws are implemented not for the single person or the one-time circumstance, but instead law is a common precept applicable to a community of men.[25] It is for the multitude that laws exist, because laws for the community are nothing more than the social sum of its members. Law, particularly the human variety, "is framed for the multitude of beings."[26] Law is equated with the happiness in both individual and culture. If lacking a communal component, the enactment would be "devoid of the nature of law."[27]

Law as Good and End

The concept of the *good*, rests heavily in Thomistic jurisprudence, whether temporal, temporary ones, or the ultimate good, the penultimate end of man – God, holistic in style, universal in approach, Thomistic law pulls in all that is good, beautiful, and perfect and finds final solace only in the beatific vision. Thomistic jurisprudence embraces more than the functionality of utilitarianism, the moral artificiality of Marxism,[28] or the vacuousness of secular humanism. A theory of law, so says St. Thomas, is loftier, rising above "prejudice and passion,"[29] and fixing "upon eternal reasons to reaffirm a forgotten truth, formulate a new principle, or overturn an established error."[30]

To be consistent with reason, man seeks perfection in every

category of life. He or she can will otherwise, but in the intricate and incomprehensible act of creation itself, God could not fashion a being who would command his or her own destruction. Since the Creator is all-good, so too the creatures molded in his image. These ideas will be more easily understood in the context of Aquinas' various kinds of law, specifically the *eternal*, *natural*, *divine*, and *human*. Man's reason, the artifice of law itself, can readily discover these ends. Perfect, unreserved happiness resides only in the splendor of divine perfection. "Perfect orderliness,"[31] as Chroust terms it, is "declaratory of the *summum bonum*, that is, of God."[32]

At every level of Thomistic thinking, legal or otherwise, God is the ultimate end of the reasoning, intellectual creature. St. Thomas urges us, "Now, from what has been seen earlier, it is established that God is the ultimate end of the whole of things; that an intellectual nature alone attains to Him in Himself, that is by knowing and loving Him, as is evident from what has been said."[33]

The Various Kinds of Law

To fathom Thomistic jurisprudence correctly, teleologically one must engage the concept of "law." Positivism, the idea that laws are laws because of promulgation, will not do. St. Thomas, impressed with the power of human law, though aware of its limitations, designs a multi-tiered construct, a hierarchical architectetonic of laws in four categories: the *eternal*, the *natural*, the *divine*, and the *human*. These four types exist independently yet dependently, distinct yet unified and integrated. Succinctly put, the hierarchy implies unity, but is dedicated to a priority of one type of law over the others. An elementary depiction would be as shown.

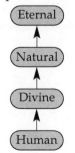

In the plan of God, the higher law descends to the lower law. Thomas sees lower forms of the law as *derived* from the higher form.

This "derivative"[34] quality commences with the eternal law, the Divine exemplar which is the blueprint for the universe and its law. Divine revelation, centrally exposed in biblical instruction, gives clarification to the people of God. Creation, especially the rational variety, participates in the eternal law by and through the natural law. Positive laws, the promulgations of man, are a necessary component for a civil society. Unified and interdependent in design, Thomistic law is complicated yet elementary. At its peak, God's eternal law watches over the other categories. "The exemplar of divine Wisdom is the eternal law,"[35] Thomas relates, and as a result "all laws proceed from the eternal law."[36]

At the human level, each derives its legitimacy from its superior counterpart. A judge, jurist, lawmaker and lawyer cannot differentiate or chop-up their legal inquiry, *e.g.*, forgetting man's natural inclination in a case of sodomy; proclaiming a humanistic notion of individual rights at the expense of common welfare; enacting a statute, interpreting a case, applying a principle, without regard for spiritual, moral, or revelatory considerations. Pure functionalism, legal emotivism, or subjectivism lack the larger framework advanced by St. Thomas. Within the *Treatise on Law*, St. Thomas offers a series of interlocking and interdependent categories of law – each form gauged in its relationship to the others before legal action will have legitimacy. The clamor of the crowd and weeping and gnashing of the individual will not suffice.

The Eternal Law

At the pinnacle in Thomistic jurisprudence is the *eternal* law of God, the rational architect of the universe and its creatures. God, as author and architect, expresses perfection, omniscience, and pure thought. God, by and through his *eternal law*, fashions an exemplar for man and his universe. The *eternal law*, as Gilson urges, is that which "makes us what we are."[37] The *lex aeterna* is the blueprint for an ordered existence, the benchmark for perfection in every facet of existence. It is "the objective and absolute *a priori* of everything that may properly be called a rule and a measure."[38]

In calling God's law the "supreme exemplar,"[39] Aquinas foundationally sets the basis for all legal practice and theory in this perennial, permanent, and immutable dimension. God, the artist and the craftsman, makes only good things, and as a result, molds creatures with lawful inclinations and components. Aquinas characterizes objects or beings by the "emanation"[40] from God's being, containing or being the law itself and the "extensiveness" of God's influence on reality itself. The perfection of God is not an unbridgeable valley, due to God's creative relationship with his authorship of the world. Creation possesses an artistic or demonstrative quality that inevitably and intimately bonds Creator with the created. The Divine God moves "all things to their due end,"[41] and "bears the character of law."[42]

The perfect God naturally has a perfect legal constitution, though His complete content and subject matter are unknowable to temporal species like man. The *eternal law* is incapable of promulgation since such promulgation is *a priori* and self-evident.[43] Thomas recognizes the human inadequacy of knowing directly and primarily what the eternal actually is – since the law is God Himself. What is irrefutable is that only God knows his own eternal law in its fullness. As imperfect beings, we can struggle only to know the effects of the eternal law. Thomas holds that we "cannot know the things that are of God as they are in themselves; but they are made known to us in their effects, according to *Rom. 1. 20: The invisible things of God . . . are clearly seen, being understood by the things that are made.*"[44]

Later on, man will get closer to knowing these effects by nature's instructions on the norms for human activity. St. Thomas is wise enough to equate the eternal law of God with that of God Himself. All that is created by God, "whether contingent or necessary, is subject to the eternal law."[45] God's law is the supreme norm for all living beings and creation. Governance of the universe by God imputes a law of operations. Thomas simultaneously uses the term "government" when God is described as "the ruler of the universe."[46] This rule has the quality of and the "nature of a law."[47]

When St. Thomas queries whether all human affairs are subject to the eternal law, only an answer in the affirmative is possible. Even the wicked and the perverse are subject to the eternal law. Even the "blessed and the damned are under the eternal law."[48] Even the ignorant cannot disavow some knowledge of the eternal law since their being still reflects the Creator by its effects. Even the lustful and the slaves of flesh cannot "dominate"[49] and destroy the good of one's nature, for "there remains in man the inclination to do the things which belong to the eternal law."[50] Nothing and no one can evade the eternal law. The eternal law, residing within, or more accurately inherently within, the God of creation, is the measure of all activity. Thomas does not hesitate calling God's law *truth* itself. At *Question 93, Article 1* he summarizes that "the divine intellect is true in itself, and its exemplar is truth itself."[51]

St. Thomas' evaluation of law cannot and does not end here; practical and pragmatic reality would not allow it. As creatures, as living agents of God's creation, simultaneously recognizing our own inadequacies to comprehend the eternal law, we need a legal benchmark that can be understood – the *natural law*.

The Natural Law

Since the human species is powerless to fully learn the mind of God and His eternal law, St. Thomas recommends a look at our very natures. Nature, in a scientific, physical sense has an order, a series of operational rules. Nature "in its purity . . . is rather like the word life."[52] Man is a creature of nature and thereby subsists of rules and operational qualities. C.S. Lewis' critical mind poses the foundational meaning of nature. "By far the commonest native meaning of *natura* is something like sort, kind, quality, or character. When you ask, in our modern idiom, what something 'is like,' you are asking for its *natura*. When you want to tell a man the *natura* of anything you describe the thing."[53] Thomas gets to the core of nature in his work, *On Kingship*, for "whatever is in accord with nature is best, for in all things nature does what is best."[54]

As author of nature, God could not and would not forge a creation of disorder and anarchy but, more predictably, infuses and imprints an orderly, lawful, natural sequence in each of his creatures. "The manifold and beautiful order of nature is the work of a designing mind of vast intelligence; and must be ultimately explained by the existence of a personal God."[55] Undoubtedly, human beings, like other beings, display natural inclinations, preferences, propensities, and dispositions that mirror the wisdom of the author. Gilson artfully offers this analysis: "Granted this, it is clear that the precepts of natural law correspond exactly with our natural inclinations and that their order is the same. Man is, to begin with, a being like all others. More particularly, he is a living being, like all other animals. Finally, by the privilege of this nature, he is a rational being. Thus it is that three great natural laws bind him, each in its own way."[56]

The term *natural law* references two critical Thomistic ideas: (1) the nature of a being itself; and (2) law as an operation of that nature. To say someone or something has a nature is to typify its very existence. Then, apply law to that nature and that nature unfolds before us – doing what it must and should do to preserve its existence; this operation signifies nature as well.[57] Nor is the natural law some changeable phenomena deposited in the creature for the moment. St. Thomas resists the effort to call the natural law a habituation because habits increase or decrease while natures are fixed.[58] Habits increase, decrease, and tend toward good things or malevolent ones. Natures are poured during a being's construction phase. A loose and impressive comparison might be this: as the eternal law is God Himself, the natural law is a mirror of really what we are as beings, because this is the eternal plan. The natural law is imprinted on man, infused into his or her nature, "written" in their hearts. How could it be otherwise when the creature reflects the Maker? Regularly found within the body of St. Thomas' work is the term "imprint" which represents the mark of the maker. The human person partakes and participates in the eternal law of God. Human beings "derive their respective inclinations to their proper acts and ends."[59] Rational creatures among all others participate most generally, Thomas remarks; "the rational creature is subject to divine providence in a more excellent way, in so far as it itself partakes of a share of providence, by being provident both for itself and for others. Therefore it has a share of the eternal reason, whereby it has a natural inclination to its proper act and end; and this participation of the eternal law in the rational creature is called the natural law."[60]

One should not think that St. Thomas' natural law is one of strict biology – it is much more comprehensive, more ambitious. A biological phenomenon would act out of necessity or pure function while Thomas' natural being moves primarily due to its rational form. Thomistic natural law fully expects reason to be the receiver of God's design. Nor is it a series of legal annotations, codifications, and enactments. More aptly, the natural law is a reflection of the whole, or as Ignatius Eschmann cogently defines the Natural Law as "not a statute enacted by the divine Legislator, but is the self-same act by which the Creator brought into being our rational nature."[61] Inclinations, tendencies, and propensities are not blank, intellectual exercises, especially since the natural-law theory of St. Thomas centrally depends upon *reason* for its discernment. Natural law for St. Thomas is more than Newtonian physics or evolutionary development. Natural law for St. Thomas is in service to the human condition, and is easily gleaned from human operation.

That water travels to its lowest point, or that bears propagate their species, is not natural-law activity as St. Thomas defines it. "It is nature itself that is, more precisely, rational nature; it is reason understood as the power of reasoning."[62] Only rational creatures possess the natural law. Natural law is about inclinations and imprints – how the human creature lives in accordance with their overall constitution. The human player living compatibly with these natural impressions, lives as the Creator intended. Natural law cannot be removed, "blotted out"[63]; moreover, it cannot be forgotten nor can its content be denied on the basis of ignorance. Natural law is the human person's *participation* in the eternal law of God. "Thus man has a natural inclination to know the truth about God, and to live in society; and in this respect, whatever pertains to this inclination belongs to the natural law: *e.g.*, to shun ignorance, to avoid offending those among whom one has to live, and other such things regarding the above inclination."[64]

From the Thomistic view, man is forged so tightly with the natural law that he cannot extricate himself from its influence. We can't even intend contrary to what we are, though we can *will* the difference – choosing evil which "is a result apart from intention."[65] Wickedness, unlawfulness, does not reside in reason or our constitution, for "such a thing is not the necessary result of what is intended; rather, it is repugnant to what is intended."[66] St. Thomas does not compartmentalize the natural law's influence on human operations but recognizes its determinative power. Every inclination in the human actor, particularly those touched or controlled by reason, deals with our natural law imprint.[67]

Those who argue its relativity, inapplicability, and selectivity as to person or precept would be at odds with Thomistic doctrine. Natural-law reasoning is scathingly critiqued by those who allege its intractability and absolutist tendencies,[68] a situation arising from language like this:

> It is therefore evident that, as regards the common principles whether of speculative or of practical reason, truth or rectitude is the same for all, and is equally known by all. But as to the proper conclusions of the speculative reason, the truth is the same for all, but it is not equally known to all. Thus, it is true for all that the three angles of a triangle are together equal to two right angles, although it is not known to all. But as to the proper conclusions of the practical reason, neither is the truth or rectitude the same for all, nor where it is the same, is it equally known by all.[69]

Critics, however, cannot fathom that natural-law reasoning insists only that a man act in conformity with what reason instructs. That there is one type of human person – the rational one – is indisputable. Reason commands as natural inclinations enunciate. In this sense, it would be ludicrous to fashion another species of man endowed with another version of reason. Therefore, in human conduct reason rules and commands the other powers, and this universal condition labels permanently the natural law.[70] This unchangeable, immutable reflection of the eternal law, this participation, albeit imperfect, by man in the eternal law, this imprint, messaging inclinations and ends for the human person, is the essence of the natural law.

The Divine Law

Thomas' recognition of the divine exemplar, the divine intellect giving rationality to the universe, and the view that God's very being is the eternal law itself, is often considered the thesis of *divine law*. *Divine law*, while having the qualities of God's rationality and plan, is not the same as the eternal law. *Divine law*, in the most elementary framework, is the Old and New Testaments, which comprise the Bible. It is easy to interchangeably term the *eternal* law the *divine*, and the *divine* the *eternal*, for common parlance often does so. Instead, one finds St. Thomas fully cognizant of the role and purpose of Scripture in the life of the Christian, and that this same Scripture has revelatory qualities. Scripture explains the mind and particular commands of a transcendent, perfect God. Additionally, the eternal, natural, and human laws, while interdependent and unified in a teleological sense, do not, according to St. Thomas, directly address the law of salvation. Thomas suggests divine law serves this end:

> [T]he end of the divine law is to bring man to that end which is everlasting happiness; and this end is hindered by any sin, not only of external action, but also of internal action. Consequently, that which suffices for the perfection of human law, viz., the prohibition and punishment of sin, does not suffice for the perfection of the divine law; but it is requisite that it should make man altogether fit to partake of everlasting happiness.[71]

It is obvious that St. Thomas is not just paying lip service as to the divine law's value in his jurisprudence. Heavily and regularly seen throughout his works is a litany of citations to Scripture passages. Jean Tonneau's essential study, *Teaching of the Thomistic Tract on Law*, mathematically computes the number of times St. Thomas utilizes scriptural references in the *Treatise on Law* at *Questions 90* through *108*. The results below present a scholar who integrates the sum and substance of Divine instruction, and simultaneously depends upon secular giants like Aristotle and Cicero. See Figure 2.2.[72]

It is nearly impossible to find a topic where he does not reference a scriptural authority. For most contemporary legal practitioners, reliance on biblical rules and authority in legal decision- making would border on the bizarre, but such a practice is perfectly compatible with a Thomistic vision incapable of segregating a life of religious experience from human activity. Without question, St. Thomas is strongly dependent on the instruction, the divinely inspired education and guidance, that the Old and New Testament provide. Man and man alone is simply incapable of operating without divine instruction for "[h]uman reason is not infallible and with the best will in the world people fall into subjective error in working out the details of right and wrong."[73]

On the other hand, it's quite apparent that St. Thomas' hierarchical coverage of law, the *eternal* to *human* legal continuum, spends less time on the divine law that its temporal counterpart, *human law*. Henle describes this portion of the *Treatise on Law* as "strictly a religious or theological one"[74] and this emphasis is not as frequently confronted in St. Thomas' jurisprudence. In fact, earlier works, like the *Summa Contra Gentiles*, appear to inaccurately distinguish between these categories of *divine* and *eternal*. At *Book III* on *Providence*, St. Thomas elevates the *divine* law more than usual, for its word is God's and its source the highest and most perfect good. The end of every law, Thomas declares, including the divine law, is to "make men good."[75] At this stage of his legal analysis, he appears to liberally interchange "eternal" and "divine" law terms. Missing within the *Summa Contra Gentiles* is the natural law's participatory role in God's eternal law, and the distinction between the revelation of God's Testaments and the law of God, the *lex aeterna*. As Thomas' thought matures, the distinction between eternal and divine will be clarified. In the *Treatise on Law*, St. Thomas unassailably depends on God's word, and its integral, central role in the life of the Christian player.

It is just this quality of "directing human conduct"[76] that makes divine law central to St. Thomas. Accepting the condition of human frailty and imperfection, realizing the historical evidence for both success and failure on the part of God's people, St. Thomas looks to scriptural instruction as a guide in a world of competing moral claims. When in doubt, God's word can and does resolve dilemmas, legal or otherwise. To assure salvation, God's divine instruction helps man "know without any doubt what he ought to do and what he ought to avoid"[77] (*homo absque omni dubitatione scire possit quid ei sit agendum et quid vitandum*).

Man's incompetency to do what is right and God's unbridled generosity in His revealing, through Scripture, the plan for human operations, the divine law anchors human kind in God's great scheme.[78] Comprehensively, Thomas inserts the divine promulgations of both the Old Law and the New, so that even though the "benefits of nature"[79] are not forfeited, the "benefits of grace"[80] are not lost through sin.

Even more persuasive is St. Thomas' argument of need as it relates to man's final end of happiness and God. Some might claim that God has equipped the human agent and instilled and imprinted in his or her nature, the blueprint for the happy life. Since we cannot comprehend the eternal law of God, understanding its effects alone, and since nature, the natural law of our operations is, for the most part, non-theological in design, St. Thomas expresses an urgency about this theological dimension. Aquinas himself argues that the principles of the natural law were "contained in the Old Law."[81] It is clear what he means. "By the natural law the eternal law is participated proportionately to the capacity of human nature. But to his supernatural end man needs to be directed in a yet higher way. Hence the additional law given by God, whereby man shares more perfectly in the eternal law."[82]

This supernatural end is just as compatible with the perception of St. Thomas on the *natural* end. Theologically, the divine law is a revealed message on how to achieve the end God intends for His creatures, and the end is not exclusively about function, machination, or bodily perfection "because it is by law that man is directed how to perform his proper acts in view of his last end"[83] (*quia per legem dirigitur homo ad actus proprios in ordine ad ultimum finem*).

Eternal happiness is an end that "exceeds man's natural ability,"[84] and the divine law fills the void.[85] St. Thomas agrees with this relational quality of the divine law since its prime aim is leading man to God, "either in this life or in the life to come"[86] (*vel in praesenti, vel in futura vita*), for the foremost purpose of the law "is for man to cling to God."[87]

At other points in Thomas' work, we decipher the instructional and educational role served by the divine law. Biblical history more than adequately manifests the need for divine scriptural reminders. The *People of God* have abbreviated memories of God's promises and God's law – so much so that "the natural law began to be obscured because of the exuberance of sin."[88]

In short, the divine law directly enunciates the faith since human reason alone cannot fully discern the things of God.[89] In both the Old and New Testaments, St. Thomas declares the plan of salvation as proclaimed by the Creator. Whether by the Old Testament's stern deterrent mentality, or the New Testament's all-encompassing charity, both scriptural domains lay out a map for salvation. The *Decalogue*, as an illustration, represents the divine law's capacity to guide, to instruct, to lead man to proper ends, and on the way giving one another their due.[90]

Divine law continually serves as a reminder to the Christian citizen and moral agent, transmitting its luminous beacon of moral truth to those "habituated to sin"[91] and "darkened as to what ought to be done in particular."[92]

Much more could be said about this component of St. Thomas' legal philosophy, but suffice it to say, the divine law is yet another reflection of God's love for His creation. Like a father to his family, St. Thomas declares the critical function of divine law in the life of the human person. "As the father of a family issues different commands to the children and to the adults, so also the one King, God, in His one kingdom, gave one law to men while they were yet imperfect, and another more perfect law when, by the preceding law, they had been led to a greater capacity for divine things."[93]

The Human Law

Those less learned about Aquinas often assume that human law is either incidental or deficient when compared to the *eternal, natural,* and *divine* law. The things of the earth are by no means as lofty or principled as the perfections of God. Nor are the legal musings of man as legislator, lawyer, and judge possibly on par with the divine or eternal promulgations. Despite the imperfection, human laws are essential to Thomas' theory of law since their content aims "at the ordering of human life . . . under the precepts of a life we have to lead."[94]

Moreover, human law maintains its integrative place in Thomistic jurisprudence because of its relation to reality, to social and political living and governance and to the advancement of temporal happiness. Undeniably, human or positive law can never be as comprehensive or as perfect as its relational superiors – the *eternal, natural,* and *divine* laws – and if its terminus and enforceability depend solely on its human, secular object, then such a law, if not today, will tomorrow exact an injustice. This inevitable tragedy that results when human law is the centerpiece of a legal system is easy enough to predict. Since *human* law is promulgated by human beings, it will always be subject to error and mistake. Nevertheless, *human* law is driving toward and is concerned with the same goods as its counterpart. Law, as previously defined, is an exercise of reason, a *rule and measure* of it. Human laws directly reflect the exercise of practical reason – assessing individual facts and circumstances and then deliberating, enacting, and infusing authority by actual laws. Human laws are not, according to Thomas, the exclusive province of the positivist. Not because man is the author of the human law, but more persuasively because man, in exercising practical reason, entwines himself with the God who fashioned him.[95] It would be grotesquely inaccurate to type Thomas' human law as isolated or independent of its legal counterparts. St. Thomas, in response to whether there is such a thing as the human law, insists on its utility and its unbridled necessity.[96] Human law is not only language, but the power to habituate, the strength to reign in the unreasonable and the untrue, a prescription for the virtues. Indeed for Thomas, "it is difficult to see how man could suffice"[97] without it.

The Necessity of Human Law

One of the most striking features of Thomas' discussion of human law is its *necessity* – a belief that human existence would fail without legal promulgations. Human beings need commands, proscriptions, and prohibitions to carry out their individual and collective enterprise. Laws serve as a series of parameters and controls for human conduct. Although human beings are fundamentally geared to the good, and by their rational nature can identify proper ends, experience delineates the value of control. Wills, passions, and appetites tug and, at times, overwhelm the rational creature who chooses conduct contrary to his nature. Indeed, St. Thomas is bold enough to assert that a morally inclined individual has little need of human law because that person already adheres to the dictates of practical reason, the mandates of the natural law, the divine law precepts, and the blueprint of the eternal law. This type of character is rare for the theory of necessity relates to the bulk of humanity.[98] Those already disposed to virtue have less need for legal regulation while those whose "disposition is evil are not led to virtue unless they are compelled"[99] (*sed quidam male dispositi non ducuntur ad virtutem, nisi cogantur*).

The necessity of human law, as St. Thomas poses, "refers to the removal of evils"[100] from the world we inhabit. Law, in the human sense, is the purifier, the fortress against the onslaught of moral barbarism. From another perspective, the necessity of human law is manifest in human activity of every sort, especially in the communal setting. Positive law involves both the *"law of nations* and *civil law"*[101] (*jus gentium et jus civile*).

Neither in anarchy nor in isolation, the human person carry out a social and political existence reliant upon law. Henle argues that human law is necessary not because of its own necessity, but because of the "state of fallen man."[102] The law is not inherently coercive, but it's consistent with all its other purposes, "directive" of what ought to be done. To be sure, law has the power to coerce and mold, but since law is a pure exercise of reason, the human actor should be comfortable with its content. Those exercising behavior in accordance with reason are willing properly and thus not in need of coercive power of the law. In this sense "the good are not subject to law, but only the wicked"[103] (*et ideo secundum hoc boni non sunt sub lege, sed solum mali*). Hence, human law is necessitous for both reasons of utility and man's current lack of perfection. It is, for lack of a better description, a libation that the virtuous can avoid and the wicked must drink.

Human Law Is Derivative

Any legal professional soon discovers that most law has a precedential legacy. Cases of first instance are temporary events, since legal pronouncements eventually attract a following. When enough people praise the decision and enough support is generated among the legal community, a legal maxim and principle is borne. To have any credibility, a law withstands the test of time and the clamor of the crowd. Good laws are not drafted in isolation, but rooted in tradition. Human law is derived from other sources including the theological and philosophical underpinnings espoused by St. Thomas. Even speeding, jaywalking, taxes, etc., have a derivative quality, especially in the justness behind their enactment. Kings, too, derive their authority from a higher power, although history is replete with examples of those who turn the crown into an anointing, who would "usurp that right, by framing unjust laws, and by degenerating into tyrants who preyed on their subjects."[104] Human law depends upon and looks to the *eternal, natural,* and *divine* laws. Using his integrative method, Thomas finds it impossible to separate human law from the natural law order so evident in rational creatures. At most, Aquinas places human law lower in his legal hierarchy because its enforceability depends upon human beings, while divine law "persuades men by means of rewards or punishments to be received from God. In this respect it employs higher means."[105] Since law is an exercise of human reason, and reason is the *rule and measure* of law, Thomas argues that human law is derived from the natural and eternal law. "Now in all human affairs a thing is said to be just from being right, according to the rule of reason. But the first rule of reason is the law of nature, as is clear from what has been stated above.[106] Consequently, every human law has just so much of the nature of law as it is derived from the law of nature."[107] Since positivism zealously excludes any rootedness beyond its promulgation, it has stripped away, gutted moral inquiry in human law analysis. Rights are based on codifications, the mutterings of "some tiny little minority of an elite,"[108] rather than inherencies or perennial truths.

The derivative relationship between the positive law and "higher" law is not one based on confrontation but one of unity and integration. Human laws that are contrary to the tenets of the natural law are, by implication, an affront to the eternal law, and not really laws in the truest sense. Radically, Thomas holds that *every law* is derived from the eternal law because of reason's role in the deliberation, and a law deviating from reason has not the nature of law in any sense.[109] A human law, inconsistent with the natural, does *violence* to the very notion of what law is and, ergo, cannot bind in conscience.[110] Neither, therefore, is it nor can it be law as popularly understood. Human laws inconsistent with the divine law receive no recognition from Thomas, since any enactment "contrary to the divine law . . . has not the nature of law."[111] Any human promulgation antagonistic to the eternal, divine, and natural laws will be an affront to any version of law and equity. To so hold is a radical error in jurisprudence. Thus, Thomas declares, "But in so far as it deviates from reason, it is called an unjust law, and has the nature, not of law but of violence."[112]

The *stamp of its ancestry* causes the Thomistic jurist to think teleologically, always searching for the ultimate end of man, that supernatural dimension in the human agent's existence, while simultaneously living in the trenches of legal practice and theory. From the foxholes will arise laws consistent with unity and derived from the natural and eternal law, or promulgations that trigger violence to the nature and essence of law. Laws are instituted, St. Thomas insists, for the average man with his many failings, not for the truly virtuous person.[113]

Thomas' just-law theory is a compelling and prophetic analysis of the human person's rights and obligations before the law, and further evidence of the law's derivative quality. Considered from various fronts, it is an account that deals with the justice, the equity of a law itself, the enforceability or obligatoriness of an unjust or just law, and the right to disobey its content. Thomas queries whether every law "binds"[114] men in conscience. If justly enacted, the answer is affirmative, since justice is consistent with reason and the perfect justice of God. Man is *not* bound to obey any unjust law because it lacks the force and nature of a law. In both contexts, the law's legitimacy is derived from a higher order. A law is just if "ordained to the common good,"[115] the divine good,[116] and nature itself. Thomas advises direct disobedience to any law "contrary to the commandments of God,"[117] since such laws are "beyond the scope of human power."[118] For laws in contravention to these principles, the human actor is not obliged or bound, neither can the state legitimately impress such laws upon its citizenry. Scholars have debated vigorously whether St. Thomas holds to the Augustinian maxim that *an unjust law is not a law at all* (*lex injusta non est lex*). Thomas exhibits more caution in this language: "That which is not just seems to be no law at all (*non videtur esse lex quae justa non fuerit*)."[119]

At *Question 96, Article 4*, St. Thomas summarizes how a law can be unjust: "(1) if it is not directed to the common good; (2) if it is beyond the authority of the law-giver; and (3) if it does not impose properly proportionate burdens."[120] In any of these cases, the law loses its force as law and cannot oblige its target. Any disregard for the eternal or natural law principles enunciated above is surely evidence of injustice. Laws crafted in derogation to the common good, an anarchy of competing, non-aligned interests replacing a common bond with "as many rules or measures as there are things measured or ruled, ... cease to be of use."[121]

Though derivative, human law is not a perfect undertaking. Human law, in order to be a sensible human exercise, cannot be expected to eradicate and suppress every act of vice or sin, since men are bound to err. Overzealously enforcing human laws will only produce social resistance and tumult. Thomas is completely opposed to a nation that enslaves its citizens by laws. Too much regulation and control will trigger a revolution of vice and even greater evils will appear. "Therefore it does not lay upon the magnitude of imperfect men the burdens of those who are already virtuous, viz., that they should abstain from all evil. Otherwise these imperfect ones, being unable to bear such precepts, would break out into yet greater evils."[122]

Human law images its author — the human person. Pragmatically, St. Thomas understands the limitations of human promulgations since no human law can plausibly be expected to stamp out human error. It is not only implausible, but presumptive, since human law lacks the power to do so. Instead, Thomas suggests a recognition of limitations in the use of human law. "Human law likewise does not prohibit everything that is forbidden by the natural law."[123]

On the other hand, the objective of human law is to look to the heavens, and to prod man toward a life of virtue. A Thomist discovers early on that law has a formidable relationship with virtue and that every human law should contribute to the advancement of individual and collective virtue. Law should foster, not inhibit, self-perfection.[124]

Human law transforms the citizenry "who live under common legal institutions into perfect citizens."[125] The law, as an instrument of the state, wishes perfection and happiness for its community. The positive or human law cannot possibly extinguish human imperfection in every case, but it can lead men gradually[126] to a life of virtue.

Summary

Before the subject of criminal law can be accurately understood, as espoused by St. Thomas, one must master his vision and definition of law. What strikes the reader new to St. Thomas is how promulgation, enactment, and the legislative process cannot be the true and singular basis for law. Law exhibits metaphysical and teleological qualities in the jurisprudence of Aquinas. Law, of whatever nature, inevitably weaves its way back to the Creator of the universe. Law is impressed in nature, rational beings, even the orderliness of the universe. For human beings, law takes on a special character – it is the rule and measure of reason. Reason contains those things necessary for the good life, and mirrors the creative process of God. The intellect possesses primary and secondary precepts on how a human being should carry out their existence. To live socially, to marry and propagate the species, to believe in God, and to preserve one's being are all imbued in reason. These laws fall under the rubric – the natural law.

All law, whether human, natural, and divine, or eternal, entwines and entangles. Human laws inconsistent with natural or eternal law deserve no recognition. Human laws are a necessity for an ordered society, but their promulgation must be mindful of natural law precepts which are part of the eternal law. Crimes are defined as such, due to their inconsistency with the eternal law of God and the natural law precepts we already understand and discern.

Notes

1 Robert Goodwin, "Aquinas Justice: An Interpretation," 63 *New Scholasticism* 275 (1989).

2. Karl Kreilkamp, *The Metaphysical Foundations of Thomistic Jurisprudence* (Washington, D.C.: Catholic University of America Press, 1939), 115.

3 J.V. Dolan, "Natural Law and Modern Jurisprudence," 16 *Laval Theologique et Philosophique* 32, 40 (1960).

4 Thomas Aquinas, *Summa Theologica*, in *Basic Writings of Saint Thomas Aquinas*, Anton C. Pegis, ed. vol. 2 (New York: Random House, 1945), II-II Q 96. (Hereafter cited as Aquinas, [title of passage], Pegis.)

5 Aquinas, *Theologica*, Pegis II-II Q 96. *See Also*: Mark R. Macguigan, "Civil Disobedience and Natural Law," 52 *Kentucky Law Journal* 347–62 (1964); Howard Zinn, "Law, Justice and Disobedience," 1990–1991 *Notre Dame Journal of Law, Ethics and Public Policy*, 899–919 (1991).

6 *See* John Finnis, "Unjust Laws in a Democratic Society: Some Philosophical and Theological Reflections," 71 *Notre Dame Law Review* 595 (1995–1996); Anthony E. Cook, "Beyond Critical Legal Studies: The Reconstruction Theology of Dr. Martin Luther King, Jr.," 103 *Harvard Law Review* 985 (1990); David Benjamin Oppenheimer, "Martin Luther King, *Walker v. City of Birmingham*, and the Letter from the Birmingham Jail," 26 *U.C. Davis Law Review* 791 (Summer 1993).

7 Igor Grazin, "Natural Law as a Form of Legal Studies," 37 *American Journal of Jurisprudence* 1, 16 (1992).

8 Noel Dermot O'Donoghue, "The Law beyond the Law," 18 *American Journal of Jurisprudence* 150, 164 (1973).

9 J.V. Dolan, "Natural Law and Judicial Function," 16 *Laval Theologique et Philosophique* 96–97 (1960).

10 Hayden Ramsey, "Demons, Psychopaths, and the Formation of Consciences," 40 *International Philosophical Quarterly* 18 (March 2000).

11 St. Thomas Aquinas, *Commentary on Aristotle's Nicomachean Ethics* 931 (Chicago: Henry Regnery Company, 1964; Notre Dame, Ind.: Dumb Ox Books, 1994), 641.

12 Gregory M. Reichberg, "Beyond Privation: Moral Evil in Aquinas's *De Malo*," 55 *The Review of Metaphysics* 775 (June 2002).

13 *See*: Gerald McCool, s.j., "Is Thomas's Way of Philosophizing Still Viable Today?" in *The Future of Thomism*, D. Hudson, D. Moran, eds. (Notre Dame, Ind.: Notre Dame Press, 1992).

14 Daniel Nelson, *The Priority of Prudence* (University Park: The Pennsylvania State University Press, 1992) 107. See also: Daniel J. Sullivan, *An Introduction to Philosophy: The Perennial Principles of Classical Realist Tradition* (Rockford, Ill: Tan Books and Pub., 1992); Bernard Beodder, s.j., *Natural Theology* (New York: Longmans, Green and Co., Ltd., 1927); Etienne Gilson, *The Christian Philosophy of St. Thomas Aquinas*, trans. L.K. Shook (New York: Random House, 1956) 266; Thomas E. Davitt, *The Nature of Law* (St. Louis: Herder, 1951) 39–54.

15 4 Thomas Aquinas, *Summa Contra Gentiles*, trans. Vernon J. Bourke (Notre Dame, Ind.: University of Notre Dame Press, 1975), Book III, part II, Chapter 114, 1.

16 3 Thomas Aquinas, *Summa Contra Gentiles*, trans., Vernon J. Bourke (Notre Dame, Ind.: University of Notre Dame Press, 1975) III-II, 115.

17 Aquinas, Gentiles III-II, 114.

18 Aquinas, Gentiles III-II, 114.

19 Aquinas, *Theologica*, Pegis I-II, Q. 90, a. 1, sed contra.
20 Aquinas, *Theologica*, Pegis I-II, Q. 90, a. 1, ad 1.
21 Anton-Hermann Chroust, "The Philosophy of Law of St. Thomas Aquinas: His Fundamental Ideas and Some of His Historical Precursors," 24 *The American Journal of Jurisprudence* 19 (1974).
22 Etienne Gilson, *The Christian Philosophy of St. Thomas Aquinas*, trans. L.K. Shook, (New York: Random House, 1956) 266.
23 Aristotle, *Phys.*, II, 9 (200a 22); Aquinas, *Theologica*, Pegis I-II, Q. 90, a. 1, c.
24 Aquinas, *Theologica*, Pegis I-II, Q. 96, a. 2, c.
25 Aquinas, *Theologica*, Pegis I-II, Q. 96, a. 1, ad 2.
26 Aquinas, *Theologica*, Pegis I-II, Q. 96, a. 2.
27 Aquinas, *Theologica*, Pegis I-II, Q. 90, art. 2, c.
28 Jeremy Bentham, *The Principles of Morals and Legislation* (New York: Hafner Publishing Co., 1948).
29 J.V. Dolan, "Natural Law & Modern Jurisprudence," 40 *Laval Theologique et Philosophique* 16 (1990).
30 Dolan at 40.
31 Anton-Hermann Chroust, "The Fundamental Ideas in 'St. Augustine's Philosophy of Law,'" 67 *The American Journal of Jurisprudence* 18 (1973).
32 Daniel Nelson appreciates this comprehensive view of law when he states, "Law in all of its manifestations derives from God's reason." Nelson 107. *See also* Chroust, "Fundamental Ideas" 67.
33 Aquinas, *Gentiles*, III-II, Ch. 112, 3.
34 St. Thomas Aquinas, *The Treatise on Law*, ed. R. J. Henle 149 (Notre Dame, Ind.: University of Notre Dame Press, 1993).
35 Aquinas, *Theologica*, Pegis I-II, Q. 93, a. 3, sed contra.
36 Aquinas, *Theologica*, Pegis I-II, Q. 93, a. 3, sed contra.
37 Gilson at 266.
38 Anton-Hermann Chroust, "The Philosophy of Law of St. Thomas Aquinas: His Fundamental Ideas and Some of His Historical Precursors," 25 *The American Journal of Jurisprudence* 19 (1974).
39 Aquinas, *Theologica*, Pegis I-II, Q. 93, a. 1.
40 Aquinas, *Theologica*, Pegis I, Q. 45, a. 3.
41 Aquinas, *Theologica*, Pegis I-II Q. 93, a. 1, c.
42 Aquinas, *Theologica*, Pegis I-II Q. 93, a. 1, c.
43 Aquinas, *Theologica*, Pegis I-II, Q. 91, a. 1.
44 Aquinas, *Theologica*, Pegis I-II, Q. 93, a. 2, ad 1.
45 Aquinas, *Theologica*, Pegis I-II, Q. 93, a. 4, c.
46 Aquinas, *Theologica*, Pegis I-II, Q. 91, a. 1, c.
47 Aquinas, *Theologica*, Pegis I-II, Q. 91, a. 1, c.

48   Aquinas, *Theologica*, Pegis I-II, Q. 93, a. 6, ad. 3.
49   Aquinas, *Theologica*, Pegis I-II, Q. 93, a. 6, ad. 2.
50   Aquinas, *Theologica*, Pegis I-II, Q. 93, a. 6, ad. 2.
51   Aquinas, *Theologica*, Pegis I-II, Q. 93, a. 1, ad 3.
52   C.S. Lewis, *Studies in Words* 37 (Cambridge: The Cambridge University Press, 1960).
53   Lewis at 24.
54   St. Thomas Aquinas, *On Kingship*, ch. II, 19.
55   Bernard Boedder, s.j.., *Natural Theology* (New York: Longmans, Green and Co., Ltd., 1927), 46.
56   Gilson at 266.
57   Alasdair MacIntyre's often cited work, *Whose Justice? Which Rationality?*, warns the critic and ally alike that the natural law is not merely a registry of pre– and proscriptions. "Obeying the precepts of the natural law is more than simply refraining from doing what those precepts prohibit and doing what they enjoin. The precepts become effectively operative only as and when we find ourselves with motivating reasons for performing actions inconsistent with those precepts; what the precepts can then provide us with is a reason which can outweigh the motivating reasons for disobeying them, that is, they point us to a more perfect good than do the latter." Alasdair MacIntyre, *Whose Justice? Which Rationality?* 194 (Notre Dame, Ind.: University of Notre Dame Press, 1988).
58   Aquinas, *Theologica*, Pegis I-II, Q. 94, a. 1.
59   Aquinas, *Theologica*, Pegis I-II, Q. 91, a. 2, c.
60   Aquinas, *Theologica*, Pegis I-II, Q. 91, a. 2, c.
61   Ignatius T. Eschmann, o.p., *The Ethics of St. Thomas Aquinas* (Toronto: Pontifical Institute of Mediaeval Studies, 1997), 187.
62   Eschmann at 166–67.
63   Aquinas, *Theologica*, Pegis I-II, Q. 94, a. 6.
64   Aquinas, *Theologica*, Pegis I-II, Q. 94, a. 2, c.
65   Aquinas, Gentiles, III-I, ch. 4, 2.
66   Aquinas, Gentiles, III-I, ch 6, 5.
67   Aquinas, *Theologica*, Pegis I-II, Q. 94, a. 2, ad 2.
68   *See* Brian Tierney, *The Idea of Natural Rights: Studies on Natural Rights, Natural Law and Church Law 1150–1625* (Atlanta: Scholars Press, 1998).
69   Aquinas, *Theologica*, Pegis I-II, Q. 94, a. 4, c.
70   Aquinas, *Theologica*, Pegis I-II, Q. 94, a. 4, ad 3.
71   Aquinas, *Theologica*, Pegis I-II, Q. 98, a. 1, c.
72   Jean Tonneau, "The Teaching of the Thomist Tract on Law," 34 *The Thomist* 31 (1970).

73 Noel Dermot O'Donoghue, "The Law Beyond the Law," 18 *The American Journal of Jurisprudence* 158 (1973).
74 Henle, *Treatise on Law* 172.
75 Aquinas, Gentiles, III-II, ch. 116, 3.
76 Aquinas, *Theologica*, Pegis I-II, Q. 91, a. 4.
77 Aquinas, *Theologica*, Pegis I-II, Q. 91, a. 4, c.
78 Rev. Patrick M. J. Clancy, O.P., "St. Thomas on Law," in St. Thomas Aquinas, *The Summa Theologica*, trans. Fathers of the English Dominican Province vol. III (New York: Benziger Brothers, Inc., 1947), 3275.
79 Aquinas, *Theologica*, Pegis, I-II, Q. 98, a. 5.
80 Aquinas, *Theologica*, Pegis, I-II, Q. 98, a. 5. Rev. Patrick M. J. Clancy, "St. Thomas on Law," in St. Thomas Aquinas, *The Summa Theologica*, trans. Fathers of the English Dominican Province vol. III (New York: Benziger Brothers, Inc., 1947) 3275.
81 Aquinas, *Theologica*, Pegis, I-II, Q. 98, a. 5.
82 Aquinas, *Theologica*, Pegis, I-II, Q. 91, a. 4, ad 1.
83 Aquinas, *Theologica*, Pegis, I-II, Q. 91, a. 4, c.
84 Aquinas, *Theologica*, Pegis, I-II, Q. 91, a. 4.
85 Gilson artistically blends this divine law and human agent into a *union*, a *unity*, a bridge spanning the chasm of the temporal and the eternal, attaching him to God by means of His love. Gilson 333.
86 Aquinas, *Theologica*, Pegis, I-II, Q. 100, a. 2, c.
87 Aquinas, Gentiles, III-II, ch. 128, 2.
88 Aquinas, *Theologica*, Pegis, I-II, Q. 98, a. 2, c.
89 Aquinas, *Theologica*, Pegis, I-II, Q. 100, a. 1.
90 Aquinas, *Theologica*, Pegis, I-II, Q. 100, a. 8, c.
91 Aquinas, *Theologica*, Pegis, I-II, Q. 99, a. 2, ad. 2.
92 Aquinas, *Theologica*, Pegis, I-II, Q. 99, a. 2, ad. 2.
93 Aquinas, *Theologica*, Pegis, I-II, Q. 91, a. 5, ad 1.
94 Aquinas, *Theologica*, Pegis, I-II, Q. 99, a. 4, ad. 1.
95 For some well-grounded discussion of positive law in Thomistic jurisprudence see Vincent McNabb, *St. Thomas Aquinas and Law* (Blackfriars, 1955) and Barry F. Smith, "Of Truth and Certainty in the Law: Reflections on the Legal Method," 30 *The American Journal of Jurisprudence* 119 (1985).
96 Aquinas, *Theologica*, Pegis, I-II, Q. 63, a. 1; Q. 94, a.3; Q. 95, a. 1, c
97 Aquinas, *Theologica*, Pegis, I-II, Q., 95, a. 1.
98 Charles Skok portrays Thomas' vision as realistic rather than pessimistic. "St. Thomas often made reference to men in their present condition. Not many men are truly virtuous or highly virtuous. Laws have to be made for the general run of the people in the state

in which they are found. This is not pessimism but realism."
Charles D. Skok, A.B., Ed.B., S.T.L., Prudent Civil Legislation
According to St. Thomas and Some Controversial American Law,
(Rome: Catholic Book Agency, 1967) 119.

99 Aquinas, *Theologica*, Pegis, I-II, Q. 95, a. 1, ad. 1.

100 Aquinas, *Theologica*, Pegis, I-II, Q. 95, a. 3.

101 Aquinas, *Theologica*, Pegis, I-II, Q. 95, a. 4, c.

102 Henle, Treatise on Law, 335.

103 Aquinas, *Theologica*, Pegis, I-II, Q. 96, a. 5, c.

104 Aquinas, *Theologica*, Pegis, I-II, Q. 105, a. 1, ad 5.

105 Aquinas, *Theologica*, Pegis, I-II, Q. 99, a. 6, ad. 2.

106 Aquinas, *Theologica*, Pegis, I-II, Q. 91, a. 2, ad 2.

107 Aquinas, *Theologica*, Pegis, I-II, Q. 95, a. 2, c. *In rebus autem humanis dicitur esse aliquid justum ex eo quod est rectum secundum regulam rationis. Rationis autem prima regula est lex naturae, ut ex supra dictis patet. Unde omnis lex humanitus posita intantum habet de ratione legis, inquantum a lege naturae derivatur.*

108 M. Gilson, Law on The Human Level: Moral Values and Moral life The System of St. Thomas, trans. L. Ward C.S.C. (St. Louis: B. Herder, 1931) 204.

109 Aquinas, *Theologica*, Pegis, I-II, Q. 93, a. 3, ad. 2.

110 Aquinas, *Theologica*, Pegis, I-II, Q. 93, a 3.

111 Aquinas, *Theologica*, Pegis, I-II, Q. 93, a. 3, ad 1. *Sic contrariatur legi Dei, et non habet rationem legis...*

112 Aquinas, *Theologica*, Pegis, I-II, Q. 93, a. 3, ad 2. *Inquantum vero a ratione recedit, sic dicitur lex iniqua, sed magis violentiae cujusdam.*

113 Aquinas, *Theologica*, Pegis, I-II, Q. 96, a. 2; Q. 69, a. 1; Q. 77, a. 1; Q. 78, a. 1, ad 3.

114 Aquinas, *Theologica*, Pegis, I-II, Q. 96, a. 4.

115 Aquinas, *Theologica*, Pegis, I-II, Q. 96, a. 4, c.

116 Aquinas, *Theologica*, Pegis, I-II, Q. 96, a. 4, c.

117 Aquinas, *Theologica*, Pegis, I-II, Q. 96, a. 4, ad. 2.

118 Aquinas, *Theologica*, Pegis, I-II, Q. 96, a. 4, ad. 2.

119 Aquinas, *Theologica*, Pegis, I-II, Q. 95, a. 2; Q. 96, a. 4

120 Aquinas, *Theologica*, Pegis, I-II, Q. 96, a. 4, c. *Dicuntur autem leges justae, et ex fine, quando scilicet ordinantur ad bonum commune; et ex auctore, quando scilicet lex lata non excedit potestatem ferentis; et ex forma, quando scilicet secundum aequalitatem proportionis imponuntur subditis onera in ordine ad bonum commune. See Damich 92.*

121 Aquinas, *Theologica*, Pegis, I-II, Q. 96, a. 2, ad 2.

122 Aquinas, *Theologica*, Pegis, I-II, Q. 96, a. 2, ad 2. *Et ideo non statim multitudini imperfectorum imponit ea quae sunt jam virtuosorum, ut*

scilicet ab omnibus malis abstineant; alioquin imperfecti hujusmodi prae-cepta ferre non valentes in deteriora mala prorumperent

123 Aquinas, *Theologica*, Pegis, I-II, Q. 96, a. 2, ad 3. *Unde etiam lex humana non omnia potest prohibere quae prohibet lex naturae.*

124 Raymond Dennehy addresses the law's ultimate aim in The Ontological Basis of Human Rights. "For, as a rational being, man attains his self-perfection by transcending the limitations of his finite, temporal self. Through the immanence of knowing, he achieves ever higher levels of reality as he identifies himself onto-logically with Being and its facets. Truth, Goodness, Beauty, and ultimately with the fullness of Being, God; and all the while he retains his own unique selfhood." Dennehy 456–57.

Chapter 2
Aquinas on Criminal Culpability

Introduction

In the present age where criminal responsibility is inexorably tied to excuse and mitigation, where criminal agents rarely admit to personal responsibility, and criminal defenses go beyond the innovative and even the bizarre, St. Thomas would not live comfortably. In a world where criminal defendants allege television and Twinkie addiction, rock music and pornography as precipitators, satanic messages and conversations with dogs, it is easy enough to see how Thomas would cringe at the avoidance of culpability. It could be argued that contemporary legal practice fosters this avoidance. With the entrenched blending of the behavioral and social sciences into America's courtrooms, the adjudication is often less about law and fact and more about personal pathology and arm-chair psychoanalysis.

In stark contrast to our current criminal law atmosphere, St. Thomas offers up the picture of the free agent, the free being, the actor who chooses and wills his events and circumstances. Essentially, the human agent engages life with a voluntariness and freedom. Therefore when a man decides to commit murder, deliberates about ways to accomplish this end, chooses the means, and then commits the crime, the action is perfectly voluntary. In a world of excuse and forbearance this may at times appear harsh and unenlightened. Upon closer inspection, one quickly discerns how brilliantly St. Thomas understands the human person.

Freedom and Criminal Culpability

At the center of Thomas' criminology rests the supremacy of the intellect, the mind, and the brain. St. Thomas holds that the intellect is the pre-eminent piece in human operations. The "intellect is the highest power of the soul."[1] Within the intellect, one knows what is true and good, and after deliberation can discern the ultimate good that all seek in human operations.[2] Couple the intellect with the will, which is about choices and means to particular ends, and you have a complex species of being. In essence, man is comprised of a soul, an intellect, a will, senses, appetites, passions, and a body. While this is ontologically crude, it is important to discover how all of these parts interweave and entwine. The intellect can be influenced by excessive passion, lust for example, which can and does lead to faulty reasoning. As Shawn Floyd holds, "passions can pose significant motivational obstacles to good action."[3] Passion, St. Thomas argues, impacts reasoning and critical thinking and causes the moral agent to justify what they know and understand to be wrong and immoral. Under the influence of passion the "good" evolves and adjusts with rationalizations that feed the sensory or the physical. Shawn Floyd most accurately described the state when the moral agent loses rational capacity.

> Passions influence reason in two ways. In one way, reason is wholly bound by passion. In such a case, a person has no use of reason, nor of will for that matter since the will's exercise relies on one's ability to reason with respect to what is good.[4]

To be good, one must be in control and guided by what the intellect holds true. Hence, St. Thomas holds that human agents must live in accordance with reason and thereby live in virtue. In this sense, virtues like temperance teach the human player how to regulate the senses and the passionate side of human operations. Reason can be consistent and correct only when guided by the moderation of temperance. Reason depends on virtue. And virtues, whether justice, courage, fortitude, chastity, or modestly, lend themselves not only to the intellectual life but the morally ordered life. A life of virtue "perfects a powers, that is, it enables the power to fulfill its end and purpose and to do so well."[5] A lack of virtue signifies predictable criminality when moral agents are driven by vices such as greed, envy, lust, sloth, and gluttony. Virtue delivers an orderly framework to live by while vice leads to chaotic crime and moral malfeasance.

"Morally good acts are means that advance man toward attainment of this goal of reason; morally bad acts take man away from this good. Good actions have generic perfection in their beings,"[6] while bad acts deconstruct or destroy the integrity of that person. St. Thomas rightly argues that a regimen of virtue will surely lead to an orderly existence.

> But the goodness of what is measured and ruled consists in its conformity to its rule . . . . evil results from a thing's not being in accord with its rule and measure, which can happen by exceeding the measure of falling short of it . . . . goodness of moral virtue consists in conformity to the rule or reason.[7]

When virtue is lacking in the human player, his thinking also suffers a deficit of moral clarity. For Thomas, virtue assures that men and women think properly and live accordingly. *Recta Ratio* – right reason – implies proper intellectual processes when weighing the suitability of conduct. "Thus in the order of reason is contained what man ought to do to be a morally good person."[8]

The will can be equally influenced by repetitive error, fear, ignorance, and a lust for pleasure. So while the will may be fundamentally good, its external influences can lead to continuous bad choices. Criminals prove this proposition repeatedly. Even so, St. Thomas finds it difficult to accept that a person can be forced to do anything against his will. Violence, he calls it, cannot really be effective against a will. John Driscoll poses this theory perfectly:

> It follows that despite violence we are held morally accountable for all acts of the will itself – for all elicited acts. But we are not responsible for commanded acts, for act performed by external faculties, which suffer violence, because in such cases, the consent of the will is absent. . . . We can force a man to kill but we cannot force him to want to commit murder.[9]

Hence our basic constitution knows the content of what is good and right, and our wills are predisposed to the correct ends, means and choices. Any truly happy person will order "his life according to reason."[10] Our blueprint for how to live is already impressed upon us by the creative design of God. Paul Glenn summarizes this interplay best:

> The will goes after what the intellect, by its practical judgment, presents to the will as a good, as an end, as something to be gone after. . . . When the sensitive appetites are permitted by the will to rise out of their proper bodily order and to exercise an influence on reason (intellect and will), they serve to move the will. . . . Thus a man who acts under stress of anger may deem fitting (that is, good, desirable), words and deeds that would not be judged fitting if he were calm.[11]

Given the rates of crime and the increasing trend toward social perversity, one can only wonder how the breakdown in our natural inclinations has occurred. Have we become so corrupted as a culture that our natural barriers to evil have melted away? Have we lost our ability to think rationally and naturally about moral choices? Has the intellect been replaced with rampant and unbridled emotivism and individualism that knows no bounds? Have we replaced perennial truths with relative demands? Are we willing to judge anything as good or bad, right or wrong, morally acceptable or not? What is certain is that thinking has been replaced with feeling, and St. Thomas's supremacy of the intellect has been vanquished by the soft science of behaviorism.

Today, most criminologists hold that the intellect is subservient to human will and desire – that human beings wish, want, desire and crave, and only then does the intellect react to the chosen path. Or just as perversely, external forces outside the human constitution cause criminality, explain its existence, and fundamentally defend the actor from his or her freely chosen actions. This portrayal accurately reflects schools of modern criminology holding ardently that human beings think only after the influences and the desires, and after the force of passions and appetites. Nothing could be further from the Thomist supremacy of the intellect over baser instincts. When succumbing to passions, the actor garners no substantive truth; in desire and want, our goods may not be accurate; in impulse and compulsion, our vision of good conduct will not be dependable. The intellect alone presents the ends we know to be good. The intellect understands the natural law – those principles common to all human agents. The intellect alone delivers the template of God's law.

For Thomas, the intellect is that point of deposit where we

know and understand what is good and how evil should be avoided. As St. Thomas comments: "Furthermore, the human mind knows the universal good through the intellect, and desires it through the will."[12] It is the locus where we discover the fundamental principles of the natural law – to seek good and avoid evil, to live in a social community, to marry, to propagate the species, and to believe in our Creator. Jan Aertsen relates how these truths find rest only in the intellect – that truth resides within the intellect if we only think on its substance.

> Truth is the end term of the process of knowing, indicates the completion or perfection of knowledge. Cognition is a process of assimilation that is completed when the similitude of the thing is known in the knower, that is, when the human mind has assimilated the object. Truth is an adequation that is realized by the intellect and in the intellect. Truth is therefore found primarily in the intellect; only secondarily it is said of things, namely, insofar as they are related to the intellect.[13]

These primordial forms of knowledge are impressed and imprinted on the human psyche. It is a place where we deliberate and issue judgments, assess and evaluate alternatives, and actualize and realize the ultimate results of the conduct chosen. It is a place where our fundamental inclinations and predispositions find solace. "In accordance with each of these inclinations, Aquinas says, practical reason forms the general principles of the natural law."[14]

While the will inherently tends toward the good, it is more readily corrupted – by passions and emotions which often can overwhelm the intellect. If free will is exercised over the wrong ends and means, the intellect will falter.[15] Citing Aristotle, Thomas relays: "And therefore the Philosopher says in Metaphysics v. Did. V. 2.) that good and evil, which are the objects of the will, are in things, but truth and error, which are objects of the intellect, are in the mind."[16]

The intellect cradles substantive truth – the substance of which cannot be blotted out from a person's mind. The intellect apprehends "universal being and truth," an "understanding of basic goods and ends" (intellectus finium),[17] while the will, the desire of the human person can choose another direction. Ralph McInerny labels this an "implicit philosophy" which is in "continuity with what everyone already knows, with the starting points or principles of theoretical and practical thinking."[18] The will is naturally receptive to this message. None of us can avoid the content. All of us can choose otherwise. Driscoll summarizes Thomas perfectly:

> When any act of ours is the product of the joint activity of intellect and will, it is said to be voluntary. It proceeds from an internal principle, the will, with an intellectual knowledge of the end of an action. Because of his gifts or reason and will, man alone, of all the creatures of this world, is capable of performing a perfectly voluntary act.[19]

Reason is the "proximate rule of morality" in human affairs.[20] Human reason is "itself a reflection of Divine reason or the Eternal Law, directing human action to the goal of life."[21]

The implications of this type of criminology are extraordinary. First, St. Thomas would be less inclined to listen to the usual panoply of excuses that rush forth in the criminal defense. From his mountaintop, the criminal agent knows the good. His intellect already has been sculpted with the essence of right and wrong. His *mens rea* has already been presumptively discovered because the criminal's mind can readily discover the "wrongfulness" of the criminality undertaken. And if human beings already know and yearn for the "good that which all things seeks whereas as evil is to be avoided,"[22] what level of toleration should be displayed by the legal system? McInerny summarizes this Thomistic conception: "Just as knowledge of good and evil cannot be completely expunged from the human mind, so the desire for the true good lurks in every act, however defective and sinful."[23]

It is in the "knowing" that the true human essence can be identified, whereby the human person "achieves higher levels of reality as he identifies himself ontologically with Being and its facets, Truth, Goodness, Beauty, and ultimately with the fullness of Being, God . . ."[24]

This type of presumption is grossly different from the contemporary criminological conception – that criminals lack the intellectual capacity to understand the nature of their conduct, or from another angle, that even if they do understand, they cannot control their course of conduct. Pathology and mitigation engages in a power grab, and it is argued, eventually subsumes the ordinary role of intellect in the human player. Stated another way, the criminal commits his crime because he or she is driven to it, or chooses the crime because his or her passion, desire, and will cripples the intellect. From this vantage point, the intellect becomes subservient to the will. In this upside down world, St. Thomas will display little if any patience, since the intellect is supreme. Since human beings are "intelligent beings . . . who have reflective self-consciousness, [and] have this inclination in an intelligent form that qualifies it as properly Law,"[25] staying on the straight and narrow is more natural than choosing the immoral pathway. And while the will may influence the intellect, and even corrupt its natural operations, the substance and content of the intellect cannot be expunged or blotted out. The intellect "is simply higher and nobler than the will."[26] For deposited in the intellect are the rules of living, the truths which lead to happiness and good.[27]

Second, we see the human actor, especially the criminal, as being a free being, endowed with free choice and free purpose. Free will and free choice are not words of puffery for St. Thomas, but indicators of our essential nature. Instead of being created as predestined robots, autonomic puppets, or another controlled entity, human beings have been blessed by true and abiding freedom in operations. From intellect to free choice and will, human beings, each and every day, make judgments about what to do and what not to do.[28] No external force or power compels us to certain conducts. John Finnis eloquently summarizes the generosity of human freedom: "That it is through one's will that one's reason has the power to move one to action and one's will is one's capacity to shape oneself by responding to reasons."[29] Humans choose freely and they do so after thinking on the parameters of conduct before them. St. Thomas compares rational man with the other animals to make his point.

> And some act from judgment, but not from free judgment; as brute animals. For the sheep, seeing the wolf, judges it a thing to be shunned, from a natural and not a free judgment, because it judges, not from reason, but from natural instinct. And the same things can be said of any judgment of brute animals. But man acts from judgment, because by his apprehensive power he judges that something should be avoided or sought.[30]

The criminal agent is first and foremost a free being, a free thinker who weighs and evaluates a series of conducts.[31] If the crime is chosen, one deduces that the intellect, which knows truth and good, has been bypassed in favor of the desire or a corrupted will. Criminals "desire against reason"[32] and are very free to choose this course of conduct. No one can force a criminal to crime. Indeed, criminality rises from a contrarian perspective in opposition to what is naturally willing and naturally good. "Aquinas thinks that all sins are instances of willing badly."[33] It might be argued that adopting a criminal lifestyle is actually a tougher road to hoe than the straight and narrow. Although St. Thomas stands rigorous against the wrongdoer, his account of culpability will call for more than mere action. He will have to be convinced that the criminal actor knows and understands the nature of his chosen conduct. As Matthew Kelly proposes: "Aquinas's views on conscience and moral agent hood should be developed along the lines that knowledge of moral quality of action and free performance of it are necessary and together suffice for a person being a moral agent."[34]

In sum, the criminal agent must not only choose his deeds freely, but he must appreciate the content and legality of that choice. There is, as Katherine Rose Hanley puts it, a consciousness of the act that implies and expressly proves the knowledge necessary for culpability.

> Considering knowledge first, St. Thomas points out that knowledge may be habitual or actual, universal or particular, speculative or practical. Moreover he notes that a judgment may be rational or perceptual. . . .
>
> St. Thomas points out that there is a genuine knowledge of what is good and right to do and conversely of what is immoral and to be shunned. The one contemplating sin knows what evil is to be avoided and what good is to be done.[35]

Just as in contemporary criminal law circles, the act and intent are co-requisites to legal proof. St. Thomas urges legal thinkers to hold accountable those who have chosen and acted with freedom and understanding.

What is clear in the writings of St. Thomas is that the criminal always understands what first principles are, but that "will" can elect another sort of rules for living. Drug users, pedophiles, violent abusers all share a similar intellectual pathology. One-on-one, an intelligent, very reasoned conversation about the criminality of their conducts can occur. Most drug addicts and pedophiles proclaim their intellectual agreement with the condemnation of the conduct. Yet, even though reason reaches this conclusion, their choice, their willed course of action, is so often contrary to this embedded information. In this fashion, they are utterly free to disregard what is true. In this manner, they turn bad into good and good into bad. These repetitive criminals deliberate, evaluate, and doggedly and persistently choose conduct that they "know and understand" to be wrong. Thomas would hold them accountable since they suffer no intellectual disorder or distress and that their criminal intent (*mens rea*) can be gleaned not only from the facts and circumstances of their crime, but their inherent understanding of good.

Free Choice and Criminal Culpability

St. Thomas poignantly addresses the question of free choice when he deals with the nature of necessity and freedom. By necessity, he means that our choices would be preplanned and pre-designated, so to speak. If this be the case, our wills would be chained to determinate action, which is contrary to the nature of freedom. Our choices cannot be tied to one option or a singular alternative, but a series of means and ways to respective ends. Freedom finds a home in a multiplicity of choices. So for the criminal element, he or she can choose to rob or not rob, rape or not rape, kill or not kill. If will was guided by necessity, there would be no freedom in any sense. St. Thomas describes the liberality of choice:

> For man can will or not will, act and not act; and again, he can will this or that, and do this or that. The reason for this is to be found in the very power of the reason. For will can tend to whatever the reason can apprehend as good. Now the reason can apprehend as good not this, viz., to will or to act, but also this, viz., not to will and not to act. Again, in all particular goods, the reason can consider the nature of some good, and the lack of some good, which has the nature of an evil. . . . Therefore, man chooses, not of necessity, but freely.[36]

If choice were not free, what need would our culture have for institutions of restraint? Why erect prisons, establish police structures, set up systems of fine and other punishment when human conduct is utterly predictable? Choice implies certain unpredictability in human affairs and surely criminal conduct, being out of the mainstream, represents this lack of predictability.

St. Thomas keenly deduces these political and communal structures that anticipate free will: "Man has free will: otherwise counsels, exhortations, commands, prohibitions, rewards and punishments would be in vain."[37] Finally, St. Thomas asserts that a rational being could not be rational without the freedom to choose. Just as animals lack the rational capacity to will anything, and operate more from instinct than any other power, a human being whose choices were pre-determined would lack the type of intellect we take for granted in *homo sapiens*.

Good and Evil in Human Action

Another thrust in St. Thomas' theory of criminal culpability relates to the nature of conduct chosen. Acts are adjudged by the object sought, the end desired, and the means to arrive at either. Some human acts are good and others evil. Further, human "acts are divided in their genus according to what is proper to man. This is to submit to the order of truth in which man can experience the undetermined, universal nature of the good."[38] St. Thomas has no difficulty being judgmental about some human conduct. This ability has been largely lost in current criminal law circles. Even the general population appears uneasy about a judgmentalism in a moral sense. The sheer volume and repetition of criminal conduct numbs the populace. What is so new about the mass murderer and the child molester? The depth, operation and depravity of 21st century criminality is a given. Sexual abuse is rampant; child molestation generously sprinkled among all the classes; violence and death, fraud and white-collar chicanery have all become part of the national landscape and communal expectation. Amber Alerts and slain high schoolers on field trips have become commonplace. As the degeneracy escalates, so does our hardening of hearts and our capacity to rationalize and tolerate even more of it. The culture accepts, as normative, ever-increasing rates of criminality. When the

numbers overflow too profusely, the legislative process decriminal-
izes. Sex with minors, obscenity, drugs, and shoplifting are but a
few examples of this descent into the world of non-judgment. St.
Thomas reminds his readers that human conduct must be adjudged
according to its object, end, and effects.

He commences with the very solid notion that not all that
humans do is good. To be certain, some human action is simply evil,
and evil conduct is that which lacks the qualities of what is good
and true in life. Evil is the privation of the good, what is lacking in
the good and in the fullness of being. Evil is "simply a privation"
and "not an essence, it is, rather, a negation in a substance."[39] St.
Thomas argues:

> We must therefore say that every action has goodness in so
> far as it has being, whereas it is lacking in goodness in so far
> as it is lacking in something that is due to its fullness of
> being; and thus it is said to be evil, for instance, if it lacks the
> measure determined by reason, or its due place, or some-
> thing of the kind.[40]

Evil lacks the qualities of perfection, the true and the good. Evil is
"deficient in act."[41] Thus, the child molester's conduct is evil
because of its extraordinary deficiency – sexual intercourse with a
non-consenting party, fornication due to sexual intercourse outside
of marriage, assault against the innocence of a child, and the emotional damage that will forever plague the victim. Gregory M.
Reichberg's cutting analysis of Aquinas on evil argues that Thomas
has even more in mind when he speaks of evil.

> Can the idea of falling always from the good, however
> refined, come anywhere close to capturing the calculation,
> the commitment, the energy, and the drive that underlie the
> most virulent projects in malfeasance? While the privation
> account might appear a reasonable strategy for explaining
> passive wrongdoing – indifference to people in grave need,
> or cooperation with injustice – the more active and dynam-
> ic forms of evil would nevertheless seem to elude its concep-
> tual net.[42]

Modern depravity appears a poor fit for this definition, but any true
understanding of St. Thomas can only lead to one conclusion – that
all that exists in creation is good – though the degrees of goodness

can and do vary greatly. Even the criminal has goodness though his activities continuously deprive the good. Even the criminal, while choosing illegal means, may wish and desire goods, despite his or her corruptions. The criminal chooses the evil of crime regardless of the "ensuing corruption of his soul, and the prospect of punishment" and willingly and freely "assumes these costs" to achieve the effects and result of crime.[43] In select cases, the activities can only be typified as intrinsically or inherently evil or characterized as "so morally disordered in themselves that they never can be justified in any circumstances or for any purpose."[44]

Criminals choose actions that cause evil. Any criminal codification worth its salt must make judgments regarding the consequences of evil choices. Criminal laws are value-driven judgments about good and evil. It is imperative that the legislator who crafts the code understand why these proscriptions not only make legal, but also moral sense. St. Thomas lays out the basis for why an act is evil and should therefore be proscribed.

Improper Object

Evil acts have in their sights improper and illicit objects, instead of the appropriate ends which all men should rightfully and justly seek. Instead of adhering to the embedded first principles of the natural law, the criminal seeks objects contrary to these ideals. The object of love, in the thought of Thomas, could not be bestiality or adultery, nor would the object of sexual intercourse simply be pleasure. Objects are what a being should strive for or properly desire. Good objects are those that advance the human person while evil objects deprive the agent of his proper ends. St. Thomas indicates that the improper object is the thing that man or woman should not love: "Now man becomes abominable to God because of the malice of his action. Therefore the malice of his action is according to the evil objects that man loves. And the same applies to the goodness of his action."[45]

Put another way, St. Thomas holds that whatever is done should be compatible with the advancement of that species or form. "In the realm of moral action . . . the wrongful [evil] act is precisely what the wicked agent aims at; this is what constitutes his objective."[46] In other words, heroin addicts cannot be engaged in good human activity if one simply reviews the effects of the human act. As the addict deteriorates into an abyss of compulsion and hallucinatory fervor, he cares little for his own body, his family or work, or for those things that will uplift and positively shape his life. It is the fix he craves, not the perfections he could achieve. The addiction is the direct byproduct of evil conduct. Hence, when drug advocates call for the legalization of all drugs, they miss the point made by St. Thomas. Evil acts produce evil and very harmful results. When this equation is met, the act should remain criminalized, for "the very proportion of an action to its effect is the measure of its goodness."[47]

The Sum of Circumstances

Another curious anomaly in current criminological reasoning is that circumstances can always explain crime and the criminal actor. It appears that St. Thomas looks at circumstances as evidence of objective evil that is not severable from the human agent that causes the chaos. Contemporary criminologists are on endless journeys trying to explain why events take place. While this is laudable, the judgment that the circumstances are evil and unacceptable should not be forgotten. There is a tendency to detach the player from the play, so to speak, in current legal thinking. St. Thomas is much more direct by not only condemning the actor, but also the circumstances sowed by his or her evil conduct. Undoubtedly, criminals lay waste to the world around them and deliver up a series of circumstances that can be properly termed "evil." Incest is not simply an act; it is just as plainly a state of life and being. Criminals ravage the landscape wherever they visit, whether the rapist or the thief, the murderer or the pedophile. Their legacy lives on in continued circumstances and within the hearts and minds of the victims who experienced their criminality. Relying on Aristotle, St. Thomas paints a very clear picture:

> The Philosopher says that a virtuous man acts as he should, and when he should, and so on, according to other circumstances. Therefore on the one hand, the vicious man, in the matter of each vice, acts when he should not, or where he should not, and so on with the other circumstances. Therefore human actions are good or evil according to circumstances.[48]

It is bad enough that the criminal actor wreaks havoc on his or her own person, and imperils their spiritual state in the eyes of God, St. Thomas states, but it is just as blameworthy to cause havoc for others in the larger, communal or familial context. Criminals spread evil in wide swathes and impacting larger constituencies than self. St. Thomas calls these effects "certain additions,"[49] and thus, the "circumstances of actions are considered in the doctrine of morals."[50]

As a result of this reasoning, St. Thomas would not accept adultery, as an example, as a mere inconvenience or minor personal matter. The evil of human action is measured in the object, the circumstances that emerge from the conduct, and the consistency with the end of the human species.

The Proper End and the Concept of Evil

Ends, in simplest terms, are what we are made for "just as the being of a thing depends on its agent and the form, so the goodness of a thing depends on its end."[51] Each and every human action "intends an end" and in natural terms, "every agent acts for a good."[52] If our agency is inclined toward the good, evil actions exist, "apart from intention."[53] "Moral acts are denoted 'good' or 'evil' principally by reference to their respective ends. Ends are to action what first principles are to thought."[54]

Our ultimate end is God, our Creator and Master of the Universe. St. Thomas never loses sight of our ultimate destiny throughout all his works. St. Thomas holds that there is an abiding and exceptional desire to "know the essence of God."[55] His commentary could not be plainer:

> It is impossible for any created good to constitute man's happiness. For happiness is the perfect good, which quiets the appetite altogether; else it would not be the end, if something yet remained to be desired. . . . Hence it is evident that nothing can quiet the will of man, save the universal good.[56]

Steven Long refers to this desire as a "natural end" and "natural desire"– the one that is simply undeniable and unquenchable.[57] He relates: "The natural desire for God then partakes of the supernatural finality without which, in this order of providence, human nature would be in vain."[58]

At the top of these, according to St. Thomas, is our perpetual desire to seek good and avoid evil, and to reach ultimate fruition in love. Jean Tonneau's wonderful examination, *The Teaching of the Thomist Tract on Law*, displays unrivaled insight into the ultimate end we all seek.

> In the domain of action, the end is the principle, and the principle of principles can only be the end of all ends, beatitude, i.e., God. No law, not even divine law, can prescribe for us the obligation of adhering to the ultimate end which is the principle of all law. In a profound sense the law does not create obligation, it discovers it; if we are already obligation, related to God, no law, not even divine law, can touch us or bind us.[59] But there are also ends that deal with human life, and whenever a conduct is contrary to those ends, St. Thomas is fully comfortable labeling it evil. What are the ends of human life? In a nutshell, these are encapsulated in the primary and secondary principles of the natural law. The natural law, as noted in an earlier chapter, is impressed into the mind and hearts of men and women. Certain things are irrefutably true about how we operate. To enumerate, humans live communally, believe in a God, marry and procreate, and preserve themselves in order to live. These goods, as John Finnis comments, represent what we are as beings. "The order Aquinas here has in mind is a metaphysical stratification: (1) what we have in common with all substances, (2) what, more specifically, we have in common with other animals, and (3) what is peculiar to us as human beings."[60]

One need only inspect human life to find order within its construct. "There is natural order of physical, chemical, and biological processes: there is the customary order of collective and habitual human practices; and there is the stipulated order of deliberate design."[61]

Thomism delivers a jurisprudence that attends to "human needs, human purposes and the human good."[62] Employing exceptional common sense, St. Thomas observes those things that all human beings predictably crave and desire. The natural law guides the human agent in the temporal sphere and provides a connection, a communion with God's eternal law – his template for proper human operations. That men and women marry, have children, wish to live, reside in communities, believe in a Deity, avoid harm, and preserve life are predictable conducts for the human species. Where the opposition arises is when these principles are applied to specific criminal law issues. Consider the following dilemmas:

✳ Suicide is Evil because it is contrary to Self-Preservation.
✳ Murder is Evil for the same reason.
✳ Abortion is Evil for the same reason.
✳ Homosexuality is Evil because it cannot lead to Procreation and Marriage.

For St. Thomas these acts are evil because none of them seek the proper end of the human agent. The homosexual, loved in the image of God, will be condemned for acts contrary to the procreative process. The patient who engages in suicide – even if of the physician-assisted variety – the murderer, and the abortionist all seek ends contrary to human fulfillment. Drugs, promiscuity, prostitution, polygamy, bigamy, child pornography, drunkenness, and a host of social and personal ills cannot reach the proper end for the human person. As St. Thomas reminds us: "Now in human actions, good and evil are predicated in relation to the reason. . . . For that is good for a thing which suits it according to its form; and evil, that which is against the order of its form."[63] Anything which stands in opposition to the good of our form will lead to ruin and turmoil in the human person. In each and every case, St. Thomas yearns for a good that causes the human person to grow and "flourish" where "virtue is primary."[64]

Summary

Practitioners and scholars of the criminal law will find the criminology of St. Thomas to be one of personal responsibility. Human agents are free beings rather than socially compelled sad figures. "Free beings" means just what it says – that human beings are culpable because of their understanding and reason. Intellect is the centerpiece of Thomistic criminality. Culpability is readily assigned because intellect reigns supreme over will, desires, senses, and appetites. The intellect already knows what is right and wrong and already possesses the rudimentary principles of the natural law. Every being seeks the good and wishes to avoid evil – desires self-preservation over destruction, and wishes to live in a collective over isolation. The intellect recognizes instantly that murder and suicide are criminal, that assault and battery, theft and fraud, rape, and child molestation are conducts forbidden under the natural-law philosophy of Thomas Aquinas. The intellect knows what our proper goods are, and fully recognizes the natural ends that human beings select. It is the passions and an over-reaching will that knocks intellect off its pedestal and causes poor choices. Crime is nothing more than a reflection of bad choices in a free-choice being. Man can do or not do, act or not act. Also, certain conduct, according to St. Thomas, lacks the good in its fullness and thereby can be labeled evil. In general, culpability is assigned to the free being who knows right and wrong and who can exercise free choice in human affairs.

Endnotes

1 Thomas Aquinas, *Summa Theologica, Basic Writings of Saint Thomas Aquinas*, Anton C. Pegis, ed. vol. 2 (New York: Random House, 1945), Q 82 Art 3.
2 *See* John E. Naus, S.J., *The Nature of the Practical Intellect According to Saint Thomas Aquinas* (Rome: Analecia Gregoriana, Liberia Editrice Dell Universita Gregoriana, 1959).
3 Shawn Floyd, "Aquinas on Temperance," 51 *The New Scholasticism* 39 (1977).
4 Floyd at 46.
5 Frank Yartz, "Virtue as an Ordo in Aquinas," *The Modern Schoolman* (March 1970), 315.
6 Vernon J. Bourkie, "Right Reason in Contemporary Ethics," 38 *The Thomist* 106, 108 (1974).
7 Aquinas, *Theologica*, Pegis Q 64, Art 1.
8 Frank Yartz, "Order and Reason in Aquinas' Ethics," 27 Medieval Studies, 475 (1975).
9 3 St. Thomas Aquinas, *The Summa Theologica*, trans. Fathers of the English Dominican Province (New York: Benziger Brothers, Inc., 1947), 3201.
10 Sister M. Rose Emmanualla Brennan, *The Intellectual Virtues*

2. Aquinas on Criminal Culpability

According to the Philosophy of St. Thomas (Washington, D.C.: Catholic University of America Press, 1941).

11 Paul J. Glenn, *A Tour of the Summa* 107–8. (Rockford, Ill.: Tan Books, 1978).

12 St. Thomas Aquinas, *On Kingship*, Translated By Gerald B. Phelan (Toronto: Pontifical Institute of Medieval Studies, 1982), 37.

13 Jan Aertsen, "The Contemporary Degate on Truth, Truth in Thomas Aquinas," *Proceedings of the Pontifical Academy of St. Thomas Aquinas* 51 (June 2001).

    See Also: Gerald A. McCool, S.J., "History, Insight and Judgment in Thomism," 27 *International Philosophical Quarterly* (September 1987).

14 Daniel A. Degnan, S.J., "Two Models of Positive Law in Aquinas," 46 *The Thomist* 1, 7 (1982).

15 *See* Donald Davidson, "How Is Weakness of the Will Possible" in *Essays on Actions and Events* (Oxford: Clarendon Press, 1994); Galvin T. Colvert, "Aquinas on Raising Cain: Vice, Incontinence and Responsibility," in 71 *Proceedings of the American Catholic Philosophical Association* 217 (1997).

16 Aquinas, *Theologica*, Benziger Q 82 at Art 3.

17 Finnis at 71.

18 Ralph McInerny, "Dialogue on Good – The Paradox of Evil," Proceedings of the Third Plenary Session, Pontifical Academy of St. Thomas Aquinas, *Doctor Communis* 72 (June 2002).

19 Aquinas, *Theologica*, Benziger, 3218.

20 Aquinas, *Theologica*, Benziger 3219.

21 Aquinas, *Theologica*, Benziger 3219.

22 McInerny at 76.

23 McInerny at 76.

24 Raymond Dennehy, "The Ontological Basis of Human Rights," 42 *The Thomist* 434, 457 (1978).

25 Vincent McNabb, O.P., *St. Thomas Aquinas and Law* 11 (London: Blackfriars, 1955).

26 Aquinas, *Theologica*, Benziger 416 Art 4.

27 See Henry Mather, "Natural Law and Right Answers," 38 *The American Journal of Jurisprudence* 297–334 (1993).

28 See Gardner Williams, "Free Will and Determinism," 38 *The Journal of Philosophy* 701–12 (1941).

29 Finnis at 70.

30 Aquinas, *Theologica*, Benziger Q 83, Art 1 at 418.

31 See Joseph Owens, C.SR.R., "Judgment and Truth in Aquinas," 32 *Medieval Studies* 1138–58.

32 Aquinas, *Theologica*, Benziger Q 83, Art 1 at 418.
33 Paul J. Weithman, "St. Thomas on Unjust Acts," *Proceedings of the Catholic Philosophical Association* 215 (1990).
34 Matthew J. Kelley, "St. Thomas and the Moral Agent," 46 *The Thomist* 312 (1982).
35 Katherine Rose Hanley, *The New Scholasticism* 497. Aquinas, *Theologica*, Benziger II-II at Q 77.
36 Aquinas, *Theologica*, Pegis Q 13 p. 285 Art 6.
37 Aquinas, *Theologica*, Pegis Q 83, Art 1 at 418.
38 Brian Thomas Mullady, o.p., "The Meaning of the Term 'Moral' in St. Thomas Aquinas," 27 *Studi Thomistici*, Pontifical Academy of St. Thomas Aquinas, Liberia Editrice Vaticana 85, 86 (1986).
39 St. Thomas Aquinas, *Summa Contra Gentiles*, trans. Vernon Bourke, vol. 4, 2nd ed. (Garden City, N.Y.: Hanover House, 1956; Notre Dame, Ind.: University of Notre Dame Press, 1975), Chapter 7 at 48
40 Aquinas, *Theologica*, Pegis Q 18 Art 1.
41 Aquinas, *Theologica*, Pegis Id.
42 Gregory M. Reichberg, "Beyond Privation: Moral Evil in Aquinas's *De Malo*," 55 *The Review of Metaphysics* 751 (June 2002).
43 Reichberg at 782.
44 John Dedek, "Intrinsically Evil Act: An Historical Study of the Mind of St. Thomas," 43 *The Thomist* 385 (1979).
45 Aquinas, *Theologica*, Pegis Q 18 Art 2.
46 Reichberg at 754.
47 Aquinas, *Theologica*, Pegis 320.
48 Aquinas, *Theologica*, Pegis Q 18 Art 3.
49 Aquinas, *Theologica*, Pegis Id.
50 Aquinas, *Theologica*, Pegis Id.
51 Aquinas, *Theologica*, Pegis Q. 18, Art 4,p 322.
52 St. Thomas Aquinas, *Summa Contra Gentiles*, Book III, Translated by Vernon Bourke, Chap. 3 at 38 (Notre Dame, Ind.: Notre Dame Press, 1975).
53 Aquinas, *Gentiles*, Chapter 4, p. 41.
54 Reichberg at 774.
55 Aquinas, *Theologica*, Pegis I-II Q3 at Art 8.
56 Aquinas, *Theologica*, Pegis I-II Q1, Art 5.
57 Steven A. Long, "On the Possibility of a Purely Natural End for Man," 64 *The Thomist* 211–37 (2000).
58 Long at 235. *See Also* R. W. Mulligan, "'Ratio Inferior' and 'Ratio Superior,'" 19 *The Thomist* 339–67 (1956).
58 Jean Tonneau, "Teaching the Thomist Tract on Law," 34 *The Thomist* 14, 65 (1970).

60 Finnis at 81.
61 James B. Murphy, "Nature, Custom and Stipulation in Law and Jurisprudence," 43 *The Review Of Metaphysics* 752 (June 1990).
62 Martin P. Golding, "Aquinas and Some Contemporary Natural Law Theories," 48 *Proceedings of the American Catholic Philosophic Association* 238, 246 (1974).
63 Aquinas, *Theologica*, Pegis I-II Q 18, Art 5.
64 Robert J. Kreyche, "Virtue and Law in Aquinas: Some Modern Implications," 5 *Southwestern Journal of Philosophy* (1974).

Chapter 3

Crimes against the Person

Introduction

ST. THOMAS' GENERAL VISION OF HUMAN INTEGRITY AND DIGNITY ALWAYS guides his thinking on whether or not it is proper to kill, injure, or harm others in a physical sense. Since the human being is crafted in the image of God, there can be no tolerable way to accept unwilling injury. Thomas relays a consistent theme by saying: "That we ought to love the nature of what God has made."[1]

St. Thomas consistently condemns physical harm against the person due to its inconsistency with the human end and purpose. Since all creatures seek perfection, however stumbling and bumbling the effort might be, harm gets in the way of growth, development, and flourishing. St. Thomas endlessly requests that all beings not only do what their intended purpose is, but do so with as much grandeur and greatness as is feasible under the conditions. St. Thomas remarks that criminal conduct against the human person works contrary to this thesis.

> By sinning man departs from the order of reason, and consequently falls away from the dignity of his manhood and in so far as he is naturally free, and exists for himself, and he falls into the slavish state of the beasts.[2]

Hence, crimes against the person are affronts to both human nature and the God that fashioned it.

Criminal Homicide

Whether an act of homicide should be termed "criminal" depends upon the circumstances. For Thomas, as in all other subject matter, his analysis avoids the absolutism he so repeatedly is accused of. As in the modern age, St. Thomas points out throughout his works the distinction between those things which are rightfully deemed illegitimate or unacceptable, and those that are unavoidable or accidental. To be a crime, the homicidal act must arise from an errant and corrupt intentionality. The human agent chooses and elects the conduct while simultaneously understanding its full import and consequence. Criminal homicide is reserved for the knowing and freely choosing being – the actor who disregards reason itself and journeys opposite its instruction. The true killer takes exception to the internal instruction of the intellect and "departs from reason."[3]

Homicide, therefore, can be assembled from a variety of definitions and circumstances. Put another way, homicide has many faces including the willful, purposeful, and intentional typology, as well as the excusable, negligent, and accidental version. Homicide means more than crime alone. Herein lies a Thomism that looks intensely at intentionality and choice – that the human agent is as responsible as his or her knowledge and understanding, the firmness of election and choice, and the precision of the deliberation leading up to the crime itself. As a result, homicide comes in many forms – the justifiable, the defensible, the mitigated, and the culpable.

Homicide by Accidental Means

In dealing with mistake, accident, and conduct resulting from chance, St. Thomas unveils a criminal philosophy that accepts notions of personal responsibility though blended with a realistic view of how human beings sometimes get into unforeseen dilemmas. Even murder can sometimes be explained. Homicide can be the result of error rather than malice, of mistake rather than willful intent and desire. Like most other things, Thomas has authored a criminal codification that looks not only to the end result and harm but the agent's intentionality. Those who kill by chance or error cannot be held accountable in the same way as the premeditated killer. Chance or accident for St. Thomas is "neither intended nor voluntary."[4] Chance happenings are not sins since these acts lack free choice and the elements of volition that impute personal responsibility. Vitoria's critical account of St. Thomas' homicide theory lays out specific examples:

> There are many contingent events, e.g., someone cuts down a tree in a grove, and by chance a passing child is killed by the fall of the tree. Is then the felling of the tree irregular? . . . [or] that someone might will to destroy the house of his enemy, and care may have been taken that no passerby be killed, but by chance a child passed by and the falling house killed him. That man does not sin by the sin of homicide; therefore.[5]

Here we encounter the pragmatic approach adopted by St. Thomas in the matter of negligent or even excusable homicide. In sum, St. Thomas recognizes that events and circumstances sometimes produce ends that no reasonable person would have rationally predicted. While St. Thomas fully accepts that part of the homicide equation has been fulfilled – namely the *actus reus* of the "killing," he stands fast against imputing culpability to those who lack the requisite intentionality. Mistake, accident, self-defense, lawful right, or privilege all negate or mitigate criminal responsibility. Put another way, homicide should not be construed as a strict liability offense, but one which has events and circumstances that thwart the imposition of criminal penalties.

From another perspective, St. Thomas appears to fully understand the nature of negligence and its relationship to homicide. Just as modern criminal codes catalog and define homicide in a negligent context, St. Thomas drafts the elements of this offense in his analysis. In the current legal setting, negligent homicide is founded when intentionality may be less direct but surely inferred. For example, drunk drivers who kill others while operating a vehicle rarely would not admit, nor is it likely to be true, that the exclusive purpose of the drinking was to kill another. Drunk drivers, for the most part, lack the clarity of intention that is common to other murder charges. In fact, drunk drivers are a repentant lot with very short memories. Yet, similar to the contemporary criminal constructions, St. Thomas would construe a negligent will and a lack of formal intention. The actor may not directly "know," although he or she "should have known." In this analysis, one quickly discovers Thomas' notion of "due care." By using a standard of due care, St.

Thomas leans towards the "should have known" end of the spectrum. In his example relating to removing an obstacle that will cause injury to another, the concept of due care emerges.

> Wherefore he who does not remove something whence homicide results whereas he ought to remove it, is in a sense guilty of voluntary homicide. This happens in two ways: first when a man causes another's death through occupying himself with unlawful things which he ought to avoid; secondly, when he does not take sufficient care.[6]

Comparatively, St. Thomas sounds very much like a civil litigation specialist when he looks to the role and occupation of the person charged. For example, doctors and other educated professionals will be held to a higher standard of due care than the average citizen. Hence, a doctor's malpractice may evolve into a negligent homicide if that professional's conduct causes the death of another. As such, it is the lack of due care which Thomas looks to in finding culpability and coupled with this, his general impression that this same professional could and should have known the eventual outcome. He relays convincingly:

> . . . if a man pursue a lawful occupation and take due care, the result being that a person loses his life; he is not guilty of that person's death: whereas if he be occupied with something unlawful, or even with something lawful, but without due care, he does not escape being guilty of murder, if his action results in someone's death.[7]

Vitoria references these failures of due care as "irregularities" of performance that may trigger a case of homicide.[8] In the case of medical professionals, Vitoria would hold accountable those professionals whose "noxious or bad medicine,"[9] caused the death of another. Despite this predilection for holding people accountable for their negligence, St. Thomas is always looking for a clean-cut line of causation. Sometimes, victims are contributors to their own destinies, and at other times, victims fail to seek help and assistance to check a smaller problem from evolving into a much larger one. Thomas is on the lookout for supervening and intervening causes for the death of another. So the small cut left unattended which matures into the infected, and more life-threatening injury, breaks up that chain of causation from the original act to the eventual demise. In other words, the irregularity must be inherently suffi-cient to cause the demise of the victim and that same victim is right-fully expected to take steps to prevent further harm.

In short, St. Thomas fully appreciates all the subtleties of negli-gent homicide. He takes for granted the act which results in death. He is less receptive to automatic imputation of culpability to the charged party. It is a given that negligent homicide lacks the depth and clarity of intentionality that appears in murder and manslaugh-ter. Indeed, there may be no intentionality whatsoever. Within this dynamic, St. Thomas weighs the concept of due care – what reason-able people can expect from one another. Due care is what is owed others as we carry out our existence. Due care constitutes the meas-ure of skill and acumen that a professional person should display. Due care comprises the measure of conduct that stays within the lines. When we stray out of the lines, negligence occurs. When someone dies as a result of that negligence, St. Thomas will no longer excuse or accept arguments of pure accident or chance. A penalty must be "inflicted on those who cause death unintentional-ly, through doing something unlawful, or failing to take sufficient care."[10]

Homicide in Self-Defense

That circumstances may cause the actor to kill to preserve one's own life has long been understood in jurisprudential circles; Thomas offers no reservations about this general principle. Self-defense, in a way, takes an inherently bad act and makes it accept-able and legitimate. Who would prohibit the right the citizen to this type of self-determination? From the Thomistic perspective, the act of self-preservation is not only natural but also obligatory. Few tenets in the natural law are as clear and undeniable as the desire to live and survive. The very designation "justifiable homicide" bespeaks this fundamental awareness regarding the primacy of life. Of all the inherencies, predispositions, and inclinations there is none more compelling or convincing as the concept of self-preser-vation. Thomas holds resolutely: "Therefore this act, since one's intention is to save one's own life, is not unlawful, since it is natu-ral to everything to keep itself in *being*, as far as possible."[11]

Thus, the inclination to live outweighs the negative effect

involving the death of another. Under usual circumstances the death of another antagonizes natural-law instincts, but the circumstances themselves create the dilemma of "double effect" – an unusual and exceptionally well-crafted resolution of moral conflicts that Western thinkers have employed in a host of ethical quandaries – from abortion to terminal life support, from theft as prevention to starvation and giving one's life for another in battle or in friendship.

With his usual clarity, Aquinas relays the doctrine of "double effect" in the analysis of homicide: "Nothing hinders one act from having two effects, only one which is intended, while the other is beside the intention. Now moral acts take their species from what is intended, not what is beside the intention. . ."[12] Self-preservation, which compels the actor to defend even at the expense of another's life, inheres to the human person. Thomas even moderately chides those who would hold to the "turn the other cheek" model in all cases, nor does he label self-preservation as some sort of charitable deficit. His assessment critiques those who would admonish the self-defender and prop up the alternative of salvation and martyrdom since avoidance of defense is "not necessary for salvation"[13] since the human agent is "more bound to take thought for his own life than for the life of his neighbour."[14]

In terms of criminal culpability, Thomas already recognizes the role necessity and duress play in the assessment of criminal action. He keenly argues that the criminal-justice model builds its edifice on the motivations and intentions of its accused and that those intent on merely saving their own lives cannot be said to wish or want the demise of another. The self-defender never really intends to kill another in a strict legal sense, but rather to insure a continued existence. The motivation, therefore, cannot be described as malevolent or willing but necessitous. John Finnis hits the nail on the head when he claims: "For in doing what I do, I need not – and must not – be intending to kill (or intend to harm.) I can – and should – be intending and choosing no more than to do what it takes to stop the attack (*repelli inuriam*)."[15]

Argued from another slant, Aquinas weighs more keenly the rationale behind the choice to kill another as compared to the act itself. The *actus reus* alone fails to encompass any murder. In Thomistic criminal reasoning the actor blends mind and act, dependent and inter-dependent in design. Moreover, St. Thomas reinforces the dualistic nature of criminal liability in Western culture, namely that a combination of mind and act are essential components of every criminal act. *Actus Reus* alone does not suffice. *Mens Rea* must be coupled with any finding of culpability. In self-defense, the "act" component of criminal guilt is demonstrated while the mental element falters.

Few thinkers of his time or ours seem so intent on peering into the deliberation and choice of the human agent. To be sure, the task of deciphering any accused's mental state is a tall order, but Aquinas thought it essential in all cases. While the actor may "appear" to be legally defensible in his or her self-defense, the actor may internally be motivated for ulterior reasons that negate the purity of the argument. Vengeance, hatred, and retaliation mitigate the self-defense claim since necessity is replaced by other agenda. Medievalist Francisco de Vitoria's 15th-century critique of the Thomistic homicide theory zeroes in on the dilemma when determining whether it is appropriate to lay in wait or secret to kill another due to fear of future harm. Inside this scenario, the necessity loses its punch and power and the motivations of the defender lack proximity to the act of self-defense. This type of defending as Vitoria puts is not "blameless."[16] Using too much force, operating from hidden agendas and motivations, avoiding and even deliberately disregarding alternative approaches to the resolution of problems, killing over trifles, especially property, all tell a story of an insincere defender who hides behind self–defense principles. Vitoria notes:

> There is a difference between choice and intention, because an intention is of that which is directly intended as an end. In this way, then, it is not lawful to intend as an end in itself the death of another, but only to do all that can reasonably done for one's own defense.[17]

St. Thomas notes that it is lawful "to repel force by force"[18] as long as the reaction does not exceed the potential harm. As in any analysis of justice, Thomas, like his Philosopher idol Aristotle, yearns for equilibrium and reciprocity. The legitimacy of self-defense not only depends on the intention, motivation, and reason of the defender but also its suitability. That force may be met by force should be tempered with a *quid pro quo* critique. How much force is necessary? Is the reactive force in excess of what is necessary to preserve one's life? Is the force in self-defense proportionate to the force exerted by the malefactor? Just as Aristotle yearned for balance in human affairs, Thomas ardently desires an identical reciprocity in human affairs. The legality of self-defense will depend on not only its need but also just as compellingly its method. Thomas condemns the defender who goes too far: "Wherefore, if a man uses, in self-defense, more than necessary violence, it will be unlawful; whereas if he repels force with moderation, his defense shall be lawful."

Abortion and Infanticide

St. Thomas authors a very unique and often times provocative argument on the illegitimacy of abortion. In general, his position is clear and unequivocal.

> He that strikes a woman with child does something unlawful: wherefore if there results the death of the woman or of the animated fetus, he will not be excused from homicide, especially seeing that death is the natural result of such a blow..[19]

Whether abortion was murder would depend on its timing. The term "animated" denotes the formation of the human person. Early-stage abortion would lack the evidentiary basis for a murder charge since the human fetus had yet to be truly formed. St. Thomas referred to this development as "ensoulement"[20] – that stage when the fetus took on the true shape of the human person, when a soul was deposited. Once the soul was impressed in that fetus the human being had taken shape. In rough terms, St. Thomas indicates that the first 40–80 days of so of fetal development is pre-ensoulement and as a result, no murder charge would be possible at this stage. John Doyle's translation of Vitoria's *Commentary* lays out the alternative resolution that St. Thomas provides in early–term abortion.

> It may be remarked that the abortion of an animated fetus, ... Is here regarded as homicide. This seems remarkably anticipatory of present day laws in various American states which prescribe a charge of homicide in such a case. . . . In

all probability his only questions would concern the species of sin when a fetus would be aborted prior to animation and the ecclesiastical penalties to be attached to abortion at different stages of fetal development.[21]

This conclusion was obviously reached with a very crude biological understanding of human development. Neo-natal science was simply beyond his ken. However, St. Thomas firmly believed that the essential form of the human person consists of the soul which vivifies and gives life to the body. Until that soul takes shape in that body, what remains is physical form, physical mass without full humanity. Commencing with a physical deposit, Thomas will believe that the human person develops in gradations, or in "successive stages" that eventually lead to the formation of the intellective soul. The soul alone has the power to actualize the human body into human personhood. And whether the soul deposits at the date of conception or some time afterwards is the question of the day. In other words, it takes time to get there – which is in direct contrast with the instantaneous deduction of present-day pro-life advocates. St. Thomas relays:

> In the first case, the necessity of the action itself results from the form by which the agent is made actual, because in order for this kind of action to exist, nothing extrinsic, as a terminus for it, is required. Thus, when the sense power is actualized by the sensible species, it necessarily acts; and so, too, does the intellect when it is actualized by the intelligible species.[22]

If the soul provides the form for the human person, St. Thomas deduced that since semen was a physical composition, it could not transmit the qualities and content of non-corporeal soul. St. Thomas deduced that it was impossible for a material power, namely semen, to "extend its action to the production of an immaterial effect,"[23] namely the soul. As a result, the intellect – the soul – "comes from without,"[24] and exactly when it arrives is Thomas' best possible guess.[25] John Finnis concludes that Thomas operated with the available science and technology for his time and admittedly this crude biology led Thomas to inevitable findings that are in opposition to current understanding of human formation. Finnis keenly states:

It seems clear that, had he known of the extremely elaborate and specifically organized structure of the sperm and the ovum, their chromosomal complementarity, and the typical, wholly continuous self-directed growth and development of the even more elaborate and specifically organized embryo or embryos from the moment of insemination of the ovum, Aquinas would have concluded that the specifically human, rational, (sensitive and vegetative), animating form and act (soul) – and therefore personhood . . . can be and is doubtless from that moment.[26]

Of course modern pro-life advocates, depending on a very advanced biology of the human person, believe the ensoulement occurs at conception. Therefore, the modern pro-lifer deduces murder in all cases of abortion, while Thomas was wary of this deduction in the first trimester.

This reticence to apply felony charges should not be misread as tolerance or approval. When dealing with the issue of murder, St. Thomas analyzes the positive-law question more than a metaphysical principle rooted in justice. St. Thomas will hold that abortion, in all cases, except to save the life of the mother, is a practice utterly opposed to the natural law. As a result of its antagonism to the natural law, the practice will be labeled a "mortal sin" punishable by eternal damnation. The attack and physical onslaught against the body in abortion can only be described as unnatural. Since procreation is construed as the chief good derived from sexual activity, and since procreation is labeled a natural-law principle of human operations, St. Thomas will not be tolerant of conduct which will undermine the natural law.[27] Killing the innocents will never be justified in the world and thought of St. Thomas, for "we ought to love the nature which God has made, and which is destroyed by slaying him."[28]

Mayhem

The hacking off of human members – arms, legs, sexual organs, eyes, and ears, is a grotesque criminal act that St. Thomas fully explained. Similar to present codes, maiming or mayhem constitutes a graver act than any assault since it calls for the cutting off, the hacking away, the dismemberment of some appendage of the body. The *actus reus* of mayhem is the dismemberment. And by logical deduction, the act cannot be the result of mistake or accident but always the result of some willing choice. Indeed, the severity and extremeness of the act connotes a mind with a mission – one dead set on this radical biological procedure. Specific mental intent matches the *mens rea*. Outside of the specific exceptions noted below, namely public punishment and medical necessity, it is "altogether unlawful to maim anyone."[29] To maim, according to St. Thomas, is to confront the essential nature of human body, to undo its natural construction. To maim is "contrary to the particular nature of the body of the person maimed."[30]

Maiming was a common practice during his time when punishments were meted out. Thieves lost hands, rapists faced castration, and adulterers were branded. Mutilation of the members was a regular correctional reaction. The cutting off of members from the body could be and was an appropriate public infliction depending on the conduct of the accused. From his perspective, the "hacking" away of the imperfect for the sake of the perfect, was necessitous. St. Thomas uses medical language to indicate that certain parties and their members are corruptions to the common good.

> If, however, the member be decayed and therefore a source of corruption to the whole body, then it is lawful. . . ..
> Hence just as by public authority is [he] deprived of life altogether on account of certain more heinous sins, so is he deprived of a member on account of certain lesser sins.[31]

The thief's hand, the rapist's genitalia, as examples, become infectious to not only the body itself, but also the communal interest at large. St. Thomas argues that maiming is a legitimate course of action since "removal of a member may be detrimental to the whole body, it may nevertheless be directed to the good of the community."[32] From a correctional perspective, maiming can be a "punishment for the purpose of restraining sin."[33] In a biblical sense, maiming the wrongdoer is completely consistent. St. Thomas was comfortable with *lex talionis* – the "eye for eye, tooth for tooth, hand for hand, foot for foot."[34] In the larger picture, St. Thomas perceives individuals as part and parcel of the communal whole and the collective. For those who choose to corrupt the integrity of the community, the reaction will be as severe and brutal as dismemberment. St. Thomas relays this position like a surgeon:

"Since a member is a part of the whole human body, it is for the sake of the whole, as the imperfect for the perfect. Hence a member of the human body is to be disposed of according as it is expedient for the body."[35]Despite this tolerance in public cases and public imposition, the easy acceptability ends here. When private parties are involved, maiming and mayhem become acts of grave evil. When done involuntarily, there can be no allowance. A person cannot willingly choose to be the victim of mayhem. St. Thomas clearly sets out the prohibition:

"But this is not lawful for a private individual, even with the consent of the owner of the member, because this would involve an injury to the community, to whom the man and all his parts belong."[36]

Even those who claim that mayhem benefits the sinner by eliminating temptation, such as castration to remove the artifice of sexual desire, are condemned by Thomas for their extremism. Self-mutilation for the purposes of temptation and avoidance of sin is never "allowable."[37] Citing St. John Chrysostom, Thomas indicates that self-castration is never justifiable, for it is not the sexual organ that causes the crime but the intellect which weighs, evaluates, and chooses specific courses of conduct.

Nor is lust tamed thereby, on the contrary it becomes more importunate, for the seed springs in us from other sources, and chiefly from incontinent purpose and a careless mind: and temptation is curbed not so much by cutting off a member as by curbing one's thoughts.[38]

On the other hand, St. Thomas allows for exceptional individual circumstances that justify maiming. In cases of medical necessity, dismemberment may be injurious to the appendage but healthy for the body as a unit. A case of medical necessity signifies a free being who chooses rationally and who realizes that a failure to cut away a corrupted member will destroy the entire body. Just as the gangrenous amputation may save the entire leg or arm, St. Thomas readily accepts the case where the member must be destroyed to save the body as a whole. To not cut away would be irrational since the member is the "source of corruption to the whole body."[39] In this case, it is "lawful with the consent of the owner of the member, to cut away the member for the welfare of the whole body."[40]

Thus, mayhem for St. Thomas mirrors the contemporary definition since the specific intent, without justification or right, without public authority, to dismember another without consent, constitutes the elements.

Assault

In keeping with St. Thomas' general approach regarding respect for others, it would be difficult to find him tolerating assault and other bodily offenses. Surely, all confrontations, the sowing of discord, the acceleration of strife, cannot be brooked by Thomas. "In fact, it is a mortal sin in the man who attacks another unjustly, for it is not without mortal sin that one inflicts harm on another even if the deed be done by the hands."[41] Thomas uses the term "strife" a sort of whipping up a private little war between combatants to describe the hideous nature of assault. He relates:

> Strife denotes an antagonism extending to deeds, when one man designs to harm another. Now there are two ways in which one man may intend to harm another. In one way it is as though he intended absolutely the other's hurt, which in this case is the outcome of hatred, for the intention of hatred is directed to the hurt of one's enemy either openly or secretly. In another way a man intends to hurt another who knows and understands his intention. This is what we mean by strife, and belongs properly to anger which is the desire of vengeance.[42]

St. Thomas identifies the essential elements of assault in his commentaries. First, there must be a specific intentionality whereby the actor knows and realizes that the harm to be inflicted is not only desired but completely willed. The criminal agent designs and chooses the plan of attack and physical assault. "Vengeance," "anger," and other malice corroborate the element of intent.[43] The assaulter, according to St. Thomas, is "always ready to fight. . . and delights in quarrelling itself."[44]

Secondly, Thomas realizes that a substantial act, coupled with a clear intent, is just as critical. Assault consists of more than petty difference, words, or insult; St. Thomas indicates it as a "war."[45] In Joseph Rickaby's exceptional work, *Aquinas Ethicus*, he argues that the Thomistic assault is more than strife but a "hurt" is serious and "something more than putting him in slight pain."[46]

By using draconian terms like "war," "vengeance," "strife," and "hatred," St. Thomas urges the fact finder to discover an assault rooted in physical injury that is measurable. Not only does this mirror modern statutory constructions; it prophetically lays out an early test of what suffices as real, substantial, and meaningful bodily harm. In war, the stakes are high, and when Thomas employs the language of combat, we can assume that much is at stake for the body. Assault is a first-degree felony that should require nothing less. Hence, words and insults will not meet the assault evidentiary threshold. In contrast, St. Thomas calls on the legal interpreter to appreciate the substantial nature of an assault charge and its corresponding injury. Assaults, St. Thomas notes, in quoting *Galatians*, are so serious that their agents "shall not obtain the kingdom of God."[47]

Corporal Punishment and Child Abuse

Our present culture tolerates little in the way of correction in the upbringing of children. From every angle, the use of corporal punishment in the correction and behavioral control of children is frowned upon. The majority of experts in psychology, psychiatry, and child development now equate assault and battery with the use of physical discipline of children. Many jurisdictions appear ready to pounce on the parent who does not spare the rod. In this very clinical age of child rearing, St. Thomas would be out of place. For him, the physical correction of children was a duty of the serious parent. Spanking, slapping, and whipping were tools of correction, not the *modus operandi* of the abuser. In the eyes of St. Thomas, the family unit simply could not function without some level of physical control. He states, like the father of five teenage boys:

> On the other hand, the father and the master who preside over the family household, which is an imperfect community, have imperfect coercive power, which is exercised by inflicting lesser punishments, for instance by blows, which do not inflict irreparable harm.[48]

Citing *Proverbs*, "he that spareth the rod hateth his son" and "Withhold not correction from a child, for if thou strike him with the rod he shall not die,"[49] Thomas offers up a balanced policy on the use of and need for physical correction in the lives of children. Such physical correction does not amount to child abuse or assault but more aptly can be characterized as a lesson of consequence resulting from fleeting pain. Even granting his general acceptance of corporal punishment, the grant is not without limitations. St. Thomas does not condone parents who whip their children up by frenzy of fear and intimidation. Nor will he authorize the underhanded provocation of children by feigning a quarrel or generating anger based on false pretenses. Nor will he permit parents to inflict punishment without restraint. St. Thomas sets reasonable parameters by stating: "Parents are forbidden to provoke their children to anger . . . [and] inflicting blows without moderation."[50]

The parental picture that St. Thomas paints is not one of brutality. Instead, Thomas calls for moderation in the imposition of physical correction and just as critically, a malleable rather than an absolute approach. Sometimes, the punishment will not bear fruit or will cause needless harm or hurt to the child. Sometimes, St. Thomas opines, it is better to forego the physical correction and apply a "merciful forgiveness" that tempers the corrective judgment.[51] Here St. Thomas manifests his extraordinary Aristotelianism.

Summary

The act of homicide is fully examines in this chapter as well as other personal offenses. St. Thomas recognizes the diverse nature of homicidal circumstances including accidental and justifiable cases as well as the premeditated, passionate, and negligent varieties of murder. Most interestingly, St. Thomas examines the concept of due care owed others in cases of negligent homicide and whether the imposition of criminal culpability is just in all cases. In addition, Thomas' view on abortion, both from a natural-law as well as criminal perspective are covered. Readers are often surprised to discover Thomas' liberality in the first trimester as to murder. Mayhem and its grotesque dismemberment tactics are fully covered. Assault receives significant coverage especially as to the sufficiency of injury and reasonableness of the reaction.

3. Crimes against the Person

In general, St. Thomas displays exceptional understanding of the many nuances of homicide.

Endnotes

1 St. Thomas Aquinas, *The Summa Theologica*, trans. Fathers of the English Dominican Province vol. I (New York: Benziger Brothers, Inc., 1947), Q 64, Art 6, 1470.

2 Aquinas, *Theologica*, Benziger II-II at Question 64, art.3 1467.

3 Aquinas, *Theologica*, Benziger II-II at Question 64, art.3 1467.

4 Aquinas, *Theologica*, Benziger II-II Q 65, art. 8.

5 Francisco de Vitoria, O.P., *On Homicide and Commentary on Summa Theologiae II-II Q.64*, translated by John P. Doyle (Milwaukee: Marquette University Press, 1997), 205 and 207.

6 Aquinas, *Theologica*, Benziger II Q 65 art 8. 1472.

7 Aquinas, *Theologica*, Benziger II Q 65 art 8. 1472.

8 Vitoria at 207.

9 Vitoria at 207.

10 Aquinas, *Theologica*, Benziger Q 65 art 8 at 1472.

11 Aquinas, *Theologica*, Benziger Q 65 art 7 at 1471.

12 Aquinas, *Theologica*, Benziger Q 65 art 7 at 1471..

13 Joseph Rickaby, S.J., *Aquinas Ethicus: The Moral Teaching of St. Thomas* (London: Burns and Oates, Ltd, 1892), 47.

14 Rickaby, at 47–48, citing *Summa Theologica* II-II, Question 64, article 7.

15 John Finnis, *Founders: Aquinas: Moral, Political and Legal Theory* (London: Oxford University Press, 1998)

16 Vitoria at 195.

17 Vitoria at 195.

18 Vitoria at 195.

19 Aquinas, *Theologica*, Benziger, Q 65, art 8 1472.

20 Aquinas, *Theologica*, Benziger, Q 118-119 I at 575–78.

21 Vitoria at 48 n 120.

22 2 St. Thomas Aquinas, *Summa Contra Gentiles*, trans. Vernon Bourke, 2nd ed. (Garden City, N.Y.: Hanover House, 1956; Notre Dame, Ind.: University of Notre Dame Press, 1975), 88–89.

23 Aquinas, *Theologica*, Benziger Q 118 art. 2, page 574.

24 Aquinas, *Theologica*, Benziger Q 118 art. 2, page 574.

25 *See* Daniel A. Dombrowski, "Rachels, Abortion and the Seventeenth Century," 9 *International Journal of Applied Philosophy* 38 (Winter/Spring 1998).
26 Finnis at 186.
27 Aquinas, *Theologica*, Benziger Q 90 et seq.
28 Aquinas, *Theologica*, Benziger Q 64 art 6 at 1470.
29 Aquinas, *Theologica*, Benziger Q 65 art 1 at 1473.
30 Aquinas, *Theologica*, Benziger Q 65 art 1 at 1473.
31 Aquinas, *Theologica*, Benziger Q 65 art 1 at 1473.
32 Aquinas, *Theologica*, Benziger Q 65 art 1 at 1473.
33 Aquinas, *Theologica*, Benziger Q 65 art 1 at 1473.
34 *Exodus* XXI
35 Aquinas, *Theologica*, Benziger Q 65 art 1 at 1473.
36 Aquinas, *Theologica*, Benziger Q 65 art 1 at 1473.
37 Aquinas, *Theologica*, Benziger Q 65 art 1 at 1473.
38 Aquinas, *Theologica*, Benziger Q 65 art 1 at 1473 citing Chrysostom in his *Homiletics on Matthew*.
39 Aquinas, *Theologica*, Benziger Q 65 art 1 at 1473.
40 Aquinas, *Theologica*, Benziger Q 65 art 1 at 1473.
41 Aquinas, *Theologica*, Benziger Q 41, art. 1. at 1363.
42 Aquinas, *Theologica*, Benziger II-II Q 41 at art 2 at 1364.
43 Aquinas, *Theologica*, Benziger II-II Q 41 at art 2 at 1364.
44 Aquinas, *Theologica*, Benziger Q 41 1363 art 1
45 Aquinas, *Theologica*, Benziger Q 41 1363 art 1
46 Rickaby at 411.
47 Aquinas, *Theologica*, Benziger Q 41 1363 art 1 sed contra.
48 Aquinas, *Theologica*, Benziger Q. 65 art.2 at 1474.
49 Proverbs XIII at 13
50 Aquinas, *Theologica*, Benziger Q. 65 art.2 at 1474.
51 Aquinas, *Theologica*, Benziger Q. 65 art.2 at 1474.

Chapter 4
Aquinas on Sexual Offenses

Introduction

ANY SCRUTINY BY THOMAS ON SEXUAL CRIMES WILL BE TWO-PRONGED IN design. First, St. Thomas will analyze the conduct in light of its ultimate end and purpose; second, the inherent dignity of the human person. Questions as to why sexual crimes are wrong take on both criminological and spiritual contexts. In a way, the conduct is wrong for reasons far greater than the statutory construction that defines it. Sexual assault, rape, and sodomy are condemnable behaviors because they strike at the very dignity of the human person.

This is not the respect based on secular culture, or the demand for rights in a legal context, but a metaphysical vision of the human person – a vision based on God's creative power and a recognition that personhood arises from God. Sexuality plays a crucial role in the maintenance and advancement of the human species, but the context for sexuality will be tied to the marital state and procreation. Sexual intercourse is "for the welfare of the whole human race."[1] The sexual act has a specific purpose in the natural order. Sexual activity should neither be dreaded nor avoided, but engaged in "due manner and order, in keeping with the end of human procreation."[2] Crimes of rape and sodomy cannot meet this aim since their end and purpose are outside rational boundaries. Sexual activity is good, St. Thomas states:

> Now just as the preservation of the bodily nature of one individual is a true good, so too, is the preservation of the human species a very great good. And just as the use of food is directed to the preservation of life of the individual, so is

the use of venereal acts directed to the preservation of the whole human race.[3]While sexual activity, in the appropriate setting, is good, the motivations of the sexual offender are rooted in force, violence and lust. Indeed, St. Thomas proclaims that lust creates a feverish frenzy in the criminal that looses all rational moorings. Lust, St. Thomas argues, is the sowing of pleasure for its own sake and an obsession with carnal desire. Lust seeks the wanton and the debaucherous. Lust wreaks the "greatest havoc in a man's mind, yet secondarily applies to any matters pertaining to excess."[4]

When the criminal conduct of a rapist is measured, it is not procreation and family that directs choice, but a specific intent to gain sexual activity despite consent, and to exercise and exert control over the victim. Domination, not love and respect, motivates the actor. Lust perfectly promotes a warped and distorted view of sexual activity. Lust seeks the sensory and pines for the flesh - it cares not for the objects nor means of its pursuit. Aquinas relays that lust gravitates towards the lower powers rather than the higher ends of the human player. Thomas states:

> When the lower powers are strongly moved towards their objects, the result is that the higher powers are hindered and disorded in their acts. Now the effect of the vice of lust is that the lower appetite, namely the concupiscible, is most vehemently intent on its object. . ..[5]

Nothing could more keenly describe the sexual offender than an actor compelled by the "vehemence of pleasure" - that is, nothing will get in the way of this target - not reason, not truth, not goodness.

Rape

St. Thomas could not be plainer when defining rape. "Rape is unlawful sexual intercourse."[6] Within this very succinct codification, Thomas lays out the essential elements. Sexual intercourse, as commonly understood, when a penis penetrates a vagina, the *actus reus* is fulfilled. As for intent, the designation of "unlawful" indicates a lack of privilege or right and the absence of consent. As in current law, St. Thomas gets even more specific by referencing "force"- "[when] a man employs force in order to unlawfully violate a virgin. . . sometimes a maid . . . is forcibly violated."[7] St. Thomas harkens the legal scholar to be mindful of the violence of rape, or as he states "that the conditions of rape remain no matter how force is employed."[8] Holding that violence can also be the product of ruse or fraud, St. Thomas displays a sophisticated awareness of how the rapist corrals the target. Not always with the knife or other weapon, but with seduction. In a sort of anticipatory theory of date rape, St. Thomas keenly understands that rape has many faces. While the evidentiary trier surely prefers forensic proof of the force, in many cases, the victims are sometimes defrauded in ways a reasonable person could never have predicted. Seduction in the contemporary sense was long ago on Thomas' radar screen. When sexual intercourse is given in promise for marriage or engagement, and the promising party reneges, the crime is seduction. Thomas warns the reader to be wary of fact patterns totally devoid of force, but simultaneously warns of how easily the innocent can be taken advantage of. In rape, Thomas insists on something a slightly more substantive. As he notes: "The employment of force would seem to arise from the greatness of concupiscence, the result being that a man does not fear to endanger himself by offering violence."[9] His analysis of rape demonstrates a keen understanding of how human beings get caught in the web of the deceiving assailant. The seductive, using trick and inordinate persuasion, are just as capable of inflicting force as the assailant with a weapon. The young, or as Thomas labels, the "virgin," are entitled to higher levels of protection due to their innocence and age. Force can be inflicted on one less sophisticated or mature – one without experience in worldly affairs. Thomas realizes that rape is often a complicated series of facts and conditions. Black–and-white fact patterns do not easily emerge. At his time, matters of consent were often clouded by parental authority, the idea of capture in war, and contractual consideration. It would be naïve to argue that St. Thomas adopted a "feminist" perspective on the rights of women in sexual-offense law. What is indisputable is that the Thomist person was a creature authored in God's plan and as a result entitled to respect. Not the respect of human rights advocacy but the respect that honors the integrity and beauty of all things created by God. Nor would

Thomas be comfortable with the modern vision of marital rape –
where a husband's unsolicited and confrontational demand for sexual intercourse can be construed as rape. St. Thomas sees the marital state as more a series of contracts and promises rather than the
appropriate deference a husband should display when rejection
occurs. St. Thomas sees forcible sexual intercourse in marriage as
wrong and surely not an entitlement, but he resists labeling the conduct rape. Thomas relays: "The man who is just married has, in
virtue of the betrothal, a certain right in her; wherefore, although he
sins by using violence, he is not guilty of the crime of rape."[1/]

Even today, St. Thomas would have support in the legal and
academic sector. Prosecutors dread the marital rape case, and the
success of these prosecutions has been minimal at best.[11] Issues of
consent and commitment, history and past sexual conduct, promises and engagement, make the charge of marital rape most difficult
to prove. Consent undermines force and undercuts theories of violence. Does this mean that a woman cannot be sexually abused in
the marital relationship? Of course not. Thomas is astute enough to
condemn any violence in the marital relationship, but equally sharp
enough to avoid alleging rape charges in the thicket of marriage. To
the modern reformer, there can be no such distinction. "Rape is
rape" and "No means No" are attractively true but insufficient evidentiary measures. St. Thomas appears to appreciate the distinction
better than most since he understands the nature of the bargain in
marriage. By no means is his position rooted in the romantic, contemporary ideal of marital bliss. More commonly, he sees matrimony and the marital state as the product of promise and exchange, of
oath and vow, and of perpetual sacrifice for one another. With such
obligations come expectations, including the desire for sexual intercourse in light of human procreation. Yet when this very natural
inclination occurs, it must be driven with charity and love. The
rapist knows not the boundaries of love or charity. Neither does the
abusive husband who employs violence to achieve what has been
promised in the bargain. In the latter case, the sexual conduct is
driven by lust. As such, it cannot and will not be approved by St.
Thomas. Although he will sternly condemn the use of violence in
the marital setting, he will not equate forcible sexual assault with
rape in this context.

In summary, St. Thomas lays out a prophetic vision of rape statutes codified in the 21st century. First and foremost, St. Thomas highlights the essential basis of every rape charge – the use of force and violence to engage in sexual intercourse with another. Thomas cuts right to it, arguing that rape is a crime of violence. Second, rape, to be rape, must dwell on issues of consent. A lack of consent undermines the legitimacy of the sexual intercourse. He fully recognizes that sexual assault inflicts a harsher reality on its victims than other bodily assault, and that these types of offenses are especially "heinous."[12]

Third, St. Thomas reserves rape charges for those offenses involving traditional sexual intercourse – that action between the male penis and the female vagina. Fourth, St. Thomas reserves the rape victimization exclusively to women. All of these elements anticipate the classical version of rape codification.

Just as modern statutory constructions often do, oral and anal sex are usually defined outside the traditional rape category, as are other offenses employing objects, or engaging in other unnatural acts. The significance of this refined definition should not be underestimated. Here St. Thomas posits a distinct severity in rape actions – all of which arises from the potential for secondary harms such as venereal disease, unwanted pregnancies, and the loss of virginity. No other sexual offense has this capacity in total.

Given this prioritization, St. Thomas will enunciate a wide array of sexual offenses that will be fully distinguishable from the narrowly defined crime of rape. Whether the definition of rape should be so restrictive has been the subject of intense commentary in the last 50 years. Some argue that rape statutes should be gender neutral, while others claim that penetration of any bodily orifice should satisfy the intercourse standard, and many would also advocate for an elimination of the marital defense in rape adjudication.[13] St. Thomas displays little tendency to these initiatives, though he uncannily anticipates a plethora of perennial dilemmas in the law of rape:

Was the force sufficient?

Was the sexual act unlawful?

Was there consent?

Who are the parties?

What are their genders?
What type of sexual assault takes place?
Did the penis penetrate the vagina?
Was the crime committed with fraud or ruse?
Is the victim married to the offender?

In the final analysis, the codification espoused by Thomas mirrors the Model Penal Code.

St. Thomas	Model Penal Code
". . . a man employs force in order to unlawfully violate a virgin . . . sometimes a maid . . . is forcibly violated."[14]	"He compels her to submit by force or by threat of . . . death . . . injury . . . to be inflicted on anyone . . ."[15]
"The conditions of rape remain no matter how force is employed."[16]	"He has substantially impaired her power to appraise or control her conduct by administering . . . drugs, intoxicants . . ."[17]
". . . man who is just married has, in virtue of the betrothal, a certain right in her; wherefore, although he sins by using violence, he is not guilty of the crime of rape."[18]	"A male who has sexual intercourse with a female not his wife . . ."[19]
St. Thomas reserves rape charges for those offenses involving traditional sexual intercourse.	"'Sexual intercourse' includes intercourse per os or per anus, with some penetration however slight . . ."[20]
Reserves the rape victimization exclusively to women.	Reserves the rape victimization exclusively to women.

Sodomy

While the law of rape concerns itself with traditional sexual intercourse, the law of sodomy looks to sexual insertions of another variety – namely same-sex anal intercourse, and in some circles bestiality. American jurisdictions have authored an eclectic menu of conduct that would fall under the sodomy category. St. Thomas seems attuned to how all unnatural acts are part of the sodomy family. St. Thomas deals with sodomy in the larger framework of "unnatural vice."[21] Four categories of unnatural vice are lumped together, namely bestiality, "uncleanness" as to oral sex, "monstrous and bestial manners of copulation," and acts of homosexuality. Until the recent decision of *Lawrence v. Texas*,[22] where the U.S. Supreme Court struck down the definition, sodomy was equated with homosexuality.

For the Thomist, sodomy fails on multiple fronts. If the end of sexual intercourse encompasses human procreation, the act of sodomy runs counter to this end. Indeed, acts of sodomy have no other end except pleasure. Pleasure for its own sake can never be a just act in the world of St. Thomas. Pleasure must rest side-by-side with a lawful act which produces the pleasure. Human conduct must correlate to its natural purpose and operation. St. Thomas articulates his position with passion:

> Just as the ordering of right reason proceeds from man, so the order of nature is from God Himself; wherefore in sins contrary to nature, whereby the very order of nature is violated, and injury is done to God, the Author of nature.[23]

As such, sodomy is described as an unnatural vice – a "special kind of deformity whereby a venereal act is rendered unbecoming."[24] Thus, anal intercourse between two men, oral sex between two women, or copulation between man and animal, annihilate the true meaning of human sexuality. Sodomy, St. Thomas argues, is indefensible since: "First, through being contrary to right reason and this is common to all lustful vices; secondly, because, in addition, it is contrary to the natural order of the venereal act as becoming to the human race."[25] In addition, St. Thomas labels sodomy as "the greatest sin amongst the species of lust."[26] When compared to rape, seduction, adultery, and fornication, sodomy ranks as the most egregious of offenses and for good cause. Sodomy, aside from failing to meet the proper ends of the human species, directly assaults nature. For example, same-sex anal sex between two males represents a grave and most serious disregard for the natural law. St. Thomas notes: "Vices against nature are also against God. . . and are much more grievous."[27] He further comments: "Therefore since by the unnatural vices man transgresses which has been determined by nature with regard to the use of venereal actions, it follows that in this matter the sin is gravest of all."[28] Statutory constructions into the later period of the 20th century adopted a similar posture. Terms like "unnatural," "contrary to nature," and the like were very common.[29]

For most of our constitutional experience, the right of states to regulate and criminalize homosexual sodomy was a given in legislative circles. The recent U.S. Supreme Court decision of *Lawrence v. Texas*[3/] struck down nearly 3,000 years of legal tradition when Texas was ordered to eliminate its sodomy statutes. Justice Antonin Scalia tied together our legal tradition, our customs, and moral history, and lamented the change:

> State laws against bigamy, same-sex marriage, adult incest, prostitution, masturbation, adultery, fornication, bestiality, and obscenity are likewise sustainable only in light of Bowers' validation of laws based on moral choices. Every single one of these laws is called into question by today's decision; the Court makes no effort to cabin the scope of its decision to exclude them from its holding.[31]

As sodomy tests nature, and in turn insults the God who crafted it, the consequences have been striking. AIDS, STDs, decadent lifestyles, health costs, family impacts, zero birth rates are just a few of the side-effects of sodomy. It is ludicrous and almost delusional to believe that unnatural human conduct has no natural consequence. St. Thomas was well aware that those who test nature will surely pay a price, and "so in matters of action it is most grave and shameful to act against things as determined by nature."[32]

Quoting Augustine, Thomas cannot brook an act, whether consensual or not, in the form of sodomy:

> These foul offenses that are against nature should be everywhere and at all times detested and punished, such as were those of the people of Sodom, which should all nations commit, they should all stand guilty of the same crime, by the law of God, which hath not so made men that they should so abuse one another. For even that very intercourse which should be between God and us is violated, when that same nature, of which life is the Author, is polluted by the perversity of lust.[33]

Incest

Sexual intercourse between those related by blood or special affinity and proximity has historically been condemned as incest. Just as modern statutory constructions prohibit sexual activity by those bound by blood or those emotionally entangled by station in a family setting, St. Thomas shows no reservation in criminalizing acts of incest. Thomas delineates various situations in his commentary and mentions parents and children, relatives and children, as well as brothers and sisters. In each case, St. Thomas persuasively argues that sexual relations between these parties suffer from "unbecomingness."[34] He commences his condemnation by portraying the natural aversion humans possess to such activities.

> There is something essentially unbecoming and contrary to natural reason in sexual intercourse between person related by blood, for instance between parents and children who are directly and immediately related to one another, since children naturally owe their parents honor.[35]

And this unbecomingness extends to relationships of affinity, such as adoptive parent, stepfather or mother, or guardian – though this "varies" in severity when compared to relationships built on consanguinity. In either case, St. Thomas constructs a criminal proscription that mirrors the Model Penal Code which recognizes that incest emerges in both types of cases – blood and affinity.

The bond of both blood and emotion makes sexual activity a dangerous and harmful conduct for all its participants. Not only are these behaviors ruinous to individuals, they are also deleterious to the family unit and the community at large. Incest produces shame and disgrace for its victims, and allows the manipulation of those reliant upon others and trustful in a subordinate relationship. Citing Valerius Maximus, the shame of even seeing a parent naked, or to bathe with a parent, are both defined as improper behavior. Sexual intercourse with a blood relative can only be described as "unseemly" and "most prejudicial to charity."[36] Incestuous sexual relations cause "certain shamefulness inconsistent with respect"[37] for those we are related to.

Just as convincingly, Thomas argues that incest fosters a sort of insularity that would be ruinous to the social structure of a community. Incest would breed intermarriage, undermine true notions of friendship, and cause less social and human interaction with those outside the circle of the nuclear family. For example, marrying outside the nuclear line opens up new relationships and social constructs, while remaining within the incestuous circle forges much less. Inbreeding in either a genetic, social, or political sense can predictably lead to all sorts of corruption. St, Thomas indicates: "Since through a man taking a stranger to wife, all his wife's relations are united to him by a special kind of friendship, as though they were of the same blood as himself."[38]

Aside from parochialism and shame, St. Thomas offers up the idea of control and sexual parameters. Put another way, sexual conduct must have boundaries, and there is a formidable need to erect limitations to sexual intercourse. Clearly, unbridled sexual activity within the family is a recipe for insane lust and debauchery. St. Thomas sets out the strict boundary that this form of sexual activity is off-limits. Otherwise, with its acceptance, "opportunities of venereal intercourse would be very frequent and thus men's minds would be enervated by lust."[39]

St. Thomas offers no insights on the genetic rationale for criminalizing incest – probably the most frequently cited justification for prohibition in the modern setting. It is likely that this sort of biogenic thinking was foreign to the medievalist. In sum, St. Thomas posits the traditional definition of incest as being sexual intercourse with those related by blood and affinity.

Bestiality

While Aquinas never directly crafts a question relative to bestiality, his broader coverage of "unnatural sex" fully encompasses the practice. There is little if any distinction between today's legislative constructions and the ideas of St. Thomas. The sexual intercourse or copulation is so unnatural because the recipient is a beast or animal below rational man. The *Summa* enunciates a clear definition: "Secondly by copulation with a thing of undue species, and this is called bestiality."[4] Any sexual action with animals in the lower order of nature offends the Author of all creation – our Eternal God. Bestiality consists of nothing more than a grievous vice "against nature" which in turn offends God. St. Thomas differentiates these unnatural sexual crimes with a sort of continuum of depravity and gravity. Bestiality can only measured in a most depraved light. St. Thomas cogently writes: "Vices against nature are also against God . . . and are so much more grievous than the depravity of sacrilege, as the order impressed on human nature is prior to and more firm than any subsequently established order."[41] Hence, as nature has been erected, any alteration of that nature will be as condemnable as the damage caused by the unnatural act. Referencing the *Book of Genesis*, St. Thomas displays no diplomacy in his condemnation of bestiality. "He accused the brethren of a most wicked crime – that they copulated with cattle."[42] That bestiality was criminalized at the time of St. Thomas is not in dispute.

Adultery

Realizing our current laxity and almost amazing tolerance of sexual conduct outside of marriage, and with other married people, it almost seems impossible to believe that adultery was once a major criminal offense. At various stages in history, a conviction for adultery could result in the death penalty.[43] For Aquinas, adultery was a most hideous offense, since there was so much at stake. Adultery manifests not only the vice of lust, but the abject betrayal of the promise made in matrimony. Rather than a mere indiscretion or peccadillo, adultery was and is an egregious offense against one's spouse. Adultery is a "special deformity" in "contravention of the marriage compact, whether through the impulse of one's own lust, or with the consent of the other party."[44]

The adulterer displays not only a lack of chastity but also a failure of integrity. The adulterer offends his or her own integrity as well as the integrity of others. The adulterer undermines the institution of marriage and the sacrament of matrimony. The adulterer risks human procreation without the stability and dependability of the marital state. Finally, the adulterer adds to the proliferation of unwanted pregnancies and children in the community. As St. Thomas so clearly holds: "But adultery is especially opposed to matrimony, in the point of breaking the marriage faith which is due between a husband and wife."[45]

Thomas refers to the damage done by the adulterer as an assault on the "fidelity of marriage,"[46] and not exclusively to the spouse, since children are often the unwitting victims of the distressed marriage. Adultery, he claims, cannot uplift human offspring, and surely is "contrary to the good of the upbringing of his own children."[47] With his usual insight, St Thomas evaluates conduct in light of appropriate ends for the human person. Adultery delivers nothing positive toward these ends. When evaluating adultery, St. Thomas weights the impacts and implications for the common good, and discerns the negative and positive influences of human action on social institutions. In adultery, the Thomistic conclusion will not be satisfied with individualistic needs – whether the adulterer is lonely, sexually frustrated, controlled by lust and other vice. These justifications cannot provide a defensible rationalization. What happens to the rest of the world around the adulterer will be given more weight. As spouses are betrayed, children are born and abandoned, existing children live in marital turbulence, illegitimacy rates rise, and individuals become consumed with vice. St. Thomas forever appreciates the illegitimacy of adultery, the stress and strain on families and the institution of marriage. With the decriminalization of adultery St. Thomas offers up a persuasive argument for why the collective should re-examine the criminality of adultery.

Fornication

For most of Western tradition and history, fornication was criminalized. Fornication, simply defined as sexual intercourse outside the marital state, has now become normative. In a culture which freely distributes condoms and advances birth control, allows abortion into the last term, educates its young and impressionable about alleged safe-sex practices, institutionalizes sexual education, and legitimates every sort of sexual compulsion and depravity in the media, St. Thomas would appear a visitor not only from another time, but another moral dimension. While fornication statutes have disappeared from the legal landscape over the past 50 years, it is worth remembering the sense and sensibility of why these laws were such perennial players in criminal codification. Simultaneously, St. Thomas' examination of fornication will assuredly remind us why fornication was once criminalized, and maybe just as effectively, instruct us on the wisdom of his view. At the culture's present pace of sexually transmitted diseases, broken families, rates of divorce, sexual offenses, child sexual abuse, levels of teenage depression and suicide, and dysfunctional and abusive relationships, a critical account of sexual freedom may be our most salient course. St. Thomas provides erudite insight into why the road to fornication is a road to personal and collective destruction.

St. Thomas describes fornication as "simple." While it may be inappropriate to discern his true intent in the description, he couples the word simple with "mortal sin." Fornication was once a common practice in many corners of the world. Even the sophisticated cultures of Rome and Greece were quite tolerant. And in biblical times, the variety of views on sex outside of marriage can be readily gleaned from the story of God's chosen people. It was the moral framework of Jewish theology and philosophy that put the question of fornication on another plane. Instead of merely gauging the sexual intercourse between consenting adults, which fornication is, as a matter of personal choice and private option, the *Old Testament* raised the bar in moral terms. St. Thomas spends considerable time discussing fornication's moral assessment:

> For among the Gentiles, fornication was not deemed unlawful, on account of the corruption of natural reason: whereas the Jews, taught by the Divine law, considered it unlawful. The other things mentioned were loathsome to the Jews through custom introduced into their daily life.[48]

Within his discourse on fornication, Aquinas liberally sprinkles passages and references to the *Old Testament*. Some would argue that Thomas was overly theological in some his arguments, but if one is fair, Thomas, while certainly theological, reaches his conclusions with diverse authorities. In the fornication commentary Thomas mentions, Aristotle's *Politics*, Gratian's *Decretals*, Augustine's *Treatise on Marriage and Sexuality*, Peter Lombard's *Ethics*, and a host of references from *New Testament* thinkers. For his time St. Thomas was amazingly eclectic. Pressing through all of his commentary is the conclusion that fornication is lethal in effect. Despite this, St. Thomas propounds a new yet very old way of looking at this dilemma. What is clear is that the consequences outweigh the benefits. A summary of the negative consequences follows.

Illegitimacy

One indicator of cultural stress is the dramatic rise of children born out of the marital state. While crueler terms, like "bastardy," were once commonly used in the law to describe this status, and that laws of all sorts, such as estates and inheritance, lineage, etc., were less favorable to the out of wedlock child, the trend today is full tolerance. Even the term illegitimate is frowned upon. These distinctions are now deemed unnecessary, and any semblance of a distinction, a mark or a negative impression has long since dissipated. This is unfortunate in a sense, since part of the stigma attached to children born out of wedlock served as a deterrent. No one really cares today about such distinctions in status and as a result the illegitimacy rate continues on its meteoric rise.[49]

If fornication has any legacy it rests in being the precipitator of the age of illegitimacy. Indeed, not even birth control nor abortion itself appears capable of stopping this extraordinary tide of births without family, without mothers and fathers, without an economic base and without legitimacy. St. Thomas envelops fornication in a panorama of social contacts and social structures. If only it was the mere deposit of a penis into a vagina. If only it was the evaporating ejaculate deposited within the woman. While fornication may be simple, life surely is not. St. Thomas describes how fornication scales the wall of the fornicator and leaves a heap of residue.

> Now simple fornication implies an inordinateness that tends to injure the life of the offspring to be born of this union. For we find in all animals where the upbringing of the offspring needs care of both male and female, whether one or several. . . . Now it is evident that the upbringing of a human child requires not only the mother's care for his nourishment, but much more the care of his father as guide and guardian, and under whom he progresses in goods both internal and external. Hence, human nature rebels against an indeterminate union of the sexes and demands that a man should united to a determinate woman and should abide with her a long time or even for a whole lifetime.[50]

Here the genius of Thomas shines through, timeless is his suggestion that fathers are needed in families. Equally so is his suggestion that a stable environment, not a fleeting one-night stand, serves as the foundation for a child's family. In contemporary settings, one can easily discern the ravages of having no foundations whatsoever. Schools do not work, children are neglected and abused, pedophilia runs rampant, children exhibit violence and engage in high levels of adult behavior, and juvenile crime rates skyrocket.

As Thomas radically states: "The sin of fornication is contrary to the good of the human race, in so far as it is prejudicial to the individual begetting of the one man that may be born."[51] Fornication is "contrary to the love of our neighbor, because it is opposed to the good of the child to be born."[52] St. Thomas perceptively appreciates the burdens these offspring will endure due to sins and crimes of their unmarried parents. Any educator who labors in areas with high illegitimacy rates will have no argument with Thomas when he remarks: "Since it is an act of generation accomplished in a manner disadvantageous to the future child."[53]

Marriage and the Impact of Fornication

If one accepts Thomas' position that sexual intercourse has an exclusive context within matrimony alone, then fornication undermines marriage. It may be less than scientific to argue that marriage is an institution under pressure for a host of reasons – none more pressing than the expansion of sexual behavior. Aquinas wanted boundaries for sexual intercourse, and the marriage relationship was the license to that activity. When these parameters of human behavior are altered – to tolerate, allow or even sanction sexual behavior in any context, something has to give. With a 50–60% divorce rate, an increase in multiple marriages, and a dramatic surge in cohabitation before marriage, or increasing decisions not to marry at all, one can fairly deduce that the institution of marriage is under severe distress. Aquinas would hold that fornication has something to do with it. Marriage for Aquinas provides determinacy, dependability, and assurances for its participants. The world of one-night stands and cavalier sexual behavior provides the very opposite result. St. Thomas keenly urges his readers to see the connection:

> The union with a certain definite woman is called matrimony. . . . Since, however, the union of the sexes is directed to the common good of the whole human race, and common goods depend on the law for their determination . . . it follows that this union of man and woman, which we call matrimony, is determined by some law. . . . Wherefore, since fornication is an indeterminate union of the sexes, as something incompatible with matrimony, it is opposed to the

good of the child's upbringing, and consequently, it is a mortal sin.[54]

Add to this another of Thomas incredible insights – that fornication undermines future marital fidelity. A person with many partners and checkered sexual history will have difficulty staying within the bounds of commitment that matrimony demands. Sexual intercourse needs to stay within the context of a loving marriage. At all other settings sin and emptiness set in. Quoting the *Book of Tobias*, Aquinas makes the point most eloquently: "Take heed to keep thyself . . . from all fornication, and beside thy wife never endure to know a crime."[55]

Fornication and Objectification of the Human Person

One final critique of fornication rests in what the action does to the actor. Since there are no limitations or boundaries in the marital construct, fornication will alter the outlook of its participants. Most evident, due to this lack of commitment and determinate relationships, will be a capacity to sleep and leave soon after, to bed without emotion or honor, to count the conquests rather than love the party one pursues in charity. Fornication hardens the heart and leads to a tendency to objectify the sexual partner. As time passes, and the partners proliferate, there is little sense of care and even less seriousness of person. Using people for sexual gratification becomes quite easy. In a way, St. Thomas concludes, fornication actually hurts the fornicator. Interestingly Thomas deduces:

> The fornicator is said to sin against his own body, not merely because the pleasure of fornication is consummated in the flesh . . . but also because he acts against the good of his own body by an undue resolution and defilement thereof, and an undue association with another.[56]

Couple this with his observation that passions rule reason, and the fornicator is a person not operating in the rational sphere, but the emotional one. Whenever passions control reason, the human person is out of kilter. Chastity is lost in favor of prodigality and lust. Thomas calls this a "vehemence of passion" that is not readily overcome. In this context the human person fails and does not achieve the type of perfection they are capable of.

Finally, fornication destroys our spiritual integrity as well. In comparing our bodily members with those of Christ, St. Thomas appreciates the interplay between our conduct and our relationship with the Creator. Engaging in fornication is not part of the Divine plan but plainly contrary to it. Fornication "offends" God and separates us from Him.

So the fornicator is really a hapless fellow – controlled by his passions more than his reason, indifferent to others, unmindful of his obligations to marriage and offspring and at odds with his Creator. He or she expends enormous energy undermining our institutions and the collective. It is no small matter.

Bigamy

Any attack on the sanctity of marriage and disrespect for the sacrament of matrimony will be staunchly condemned by St. Thomas. Marriage is a bond and a formal unity, a joining between two consenting parties, and any action which undermines that relationship will be criminalized by St. Thomas. He describes this unity as so:

> A joining denotes a kind of uniting, and so wherever things are united there must be a joining. Now things directed to one purpose are said to be united in their directions thereto. . . . Hence since by marriage certain persons are directed to one begetting and upbringing of children, and again to one family like, it is clear that in matrimony there is a joining in respect of which we speak of husband and wife; and this joining, through being directed to some one thing is matrimony: while the joining of bodies and minds is a result of matrimony.[57]

That joining implies a unity of two persons in the bond of matrimony. Marriage provides the social and spiritual structure for a "common life in family matters."[58] Bigamy undercuts this very definition by the destruction of unity between the marital partners. Bigamy, which consists of multiple marital relationships among identical parties, destroys the historic bond and contractual promise that any marriage entails – that is to love and cherish one another till death. Bigamy creates a parallel "companionship" that operates in secrecy and fraud. Instead of the "fidelity" that each marriage rightfully insists upon, the bigamist lives in the underworld of multiple relationships, boldly breaking the promise of charity in the marital state. Bigamy, St. Thomas states, leads only to the ruination of marital integrity, and is nothing else than an indefensible irregularity. "Bigamy causes irregularity, because it destroys the perfect signification of the sacrament: which is seated both in the union of the minds, as expressed by the consent, and in the union of the bodies."[59]

This defect of marriage runs contrary to the marital ideal when marriage "requires the husband to have only one wife, and the wife to have only one husband."[60] St. Thomas also views the marital state in most spiritual terms, a holy alliance blessed by God that will devolve into lust and passion in a bigamous state. Multiple wives and husbands leads to multiple conjugal activities. Bigamy is "incompatible with spirituality, inasmuch as it makes a man to be wholly carnal."[61] The bigamous state causes the spouse to be "unwilling to be content with one wife"[62] and thusly more inclined to promiscuity and lust.

Modern statutory constructions put more emphasis on the deceit element of bigamy than Thomas does. His tact relates more to the impediment and spiritual harm that multiple marriages cause. Additionally, St. Thomas is well aware of the damage directed at children in these illicit relationships. Bigamy is "contrary to the good of the offspring"[63] since the only true and abiding marriage rests with parents that "remain together permanently."[64]

Polygamy

St. Thomas covers polygamy with moral clarity and prudential insight. While it is not surprising that he finds the practice illegitimate, his rationale is imbued with a complete recognition that all the players suffer in this scenario. His arguments tend to look exclusively at the dilemmas of multiple wives, though there is reference to multiple husbands as well. In either case, polygamy fails on various fronts. First, the practice is unjust since the disproportionality in the relationship condemns the subservient parties. In this case, the multiple wives will never receive what is due since the obligation has been spread too thin to accord any wife any justice. As St. Thomas finds, polygamy cannot "render those actions proportionate to their end."[65] Put simply, it is unnatural to expect our species, the human person, to take on more than we are intended to tackle. Polygamy, "he says, is opposed to the secondary precepts of the natural law."[66] A plurality of wives is in opposition to "nature's dictate to every animal according to the mode befitting its nature."[67]

History, custom, and experience all indicate that *homo sapiens* survive best in monogamous, marital relationships. The same could be said of children according to Thomas: "Wherefore also certain animals, the rearing of whose offspring demands the care of both, namely the male and female, by natural instinct cling to the union of one with one, for instance the turtle-dove, the dove and so forth."[68]

Second, polygamy sows confusion for not only the partners but their offspring, who cannot properly identify a mother among a series of mothers, and said confusion is utterly unnatural for the human agent. St. Thomas realizes that the "begetting" is merely the beginning step resulting from the conjugal act. This act alone does not justify polygamy and in more tragic terms cannot assure the proper upbringing of offspring. St. Thomas lucidly enunciates this failure in polygamy: "[T]he principle end of marriage is, in one respect, entirely destroyed, and in another respect hindered. For the good of the offspring means not only begetting, but also rearing."[69]

Using harsh terms, St. Thomas labels the offspring of polygamous relationships as children of "shame,"[70] not because these children earned this designation, but because of vicarious inheritance. Tolerance of contemporary out-of-wedlock children corroborates much of what St. Thomas held dear. Children without fathers and mothers suffer far more than their nuclear counterparts. Children whose parents vary by birth order and sibling cannot be as educated, as morally upright, and assecure in their self as those with identifiable mothers and fathers. Nature instructs us as does experience that traditional marriage leads to full human development. St. Thomas sets out the pastoral picture of familial tranquility.

> Now since the rearing and teaching of the children remain a duty of the parents during a long period of time, the law of nature requires the father and mother to dwell together for a long time, in order that together they may be of assistance to their children. . . . Now this obligation binds the female and her mate to remain together constitutes matrimony.[71]

Finally, polygamy cannot be lawful since it fosters fornication in the actors. If one marriage commences in legitimacy, the second and third, etc., suffer from significant defects that do not constitute the marital state. As a result, the arrangements of multiple wives are nothing more than illicit affairs properly described as fornication. As noted above, sexual intercourse outside the marital context destroys the "due relations of the parent with the offspring that is nature's aim in sexual intercourse."[72] In this sense, polygamy delivers the domino effect of other criminality in guise of fornication, adultery, child abuse, and other neglect.

Summary

Coverage of sexual offenses is both erudite and comprehensive. St. Thomas understands the cumbersome dynamics of sexual offenses. All sexual offenses are acts outside the appropriate context and driven by vice and raw violence or pleasure. The examination of lust and its effect on the criminal offender lends much to our understanding of criminal motivation. St. Thomas defines rape as current codifications do, with the concepts of force, consent, status and age fully analyzed. He also manifests a sophisticated understanding of the role of fraud, deception, and seduction in sexual offenses.

Sodomy as to homosexuality and bestiality receive significant attention. Sodomy can never be justified in the world of St. Thomas, since its chief aim is pleasure for its own sake, and from a functional perspective, procreation is a biological impossibility. Thomas' discussion of sodomy exhibits love for the sinner but no tolerance or political correctness as to the act. He characterizes these deeds as the gravest against nature and God. Incest, adultery, and fornication are critically assessed. In the former offense, St. Thomas fully appreciates the criminal actor either being related by blood or affinity. Cultural commentators would be wise to revisit the stinging analysis of St. Thomas regarding adultery and fornication.

Endnotes

1 St. Thomas Aquinas, *The Summa Theologica*, trans. Fathers of the English Dominican Province (New York: Benziger Brothers, Inc.,

1947) Q 153, art 2 at 1811.

2   Aquinas, *Theologica*, Benziger at Q 153, art 2 at 1811.

3   Aquinas, *Theologica*, Benziger at Q 153, art 2 at 1811.

4   Aquinas, *Theologica*, Benziger at Q 153, art 2 1810.

5   Aquinas, *Theologica*, Benziger at Q 153, art 5 at 1813.

6   Aquinas, *Theologica*, Benziger at Q 153, art 7.

7   Aquinas, *Theologica*, Benziger Q 154 art 7 at 1822.

8   Aquinas, *Theologica*, Benziger Q 154 art 7 at 1822.

9   Aquinas, *Theologica*, Benziger Q 154 art7 at 1822.

10 Aquinas, *Theologica*, Benziger Q 154 art7 at 1822.

11 Charles P. Nemeth, "New Jersey Prosecutors View the New Sexual Offense Statutes" *N.J.L.J.*, May 5, 1983.

12 Aquinas, *Theologica*, Benziger Q 154, art 7 at 1822.

13 Rebecca M. Ryan, "The Sex Right: A Legal History of the Marital Rape Exemption," *Law & Social Inquiry*, Vol. 20, No. 4 (Autumn, 1995), pp. 941-1001.

14 Aquinas, *Theologica*, Benziger Q 154, art 7 at 1822.

15 MPC 213.1(1)(a).

16 Aquinas, *Theologica*, Benziger Q 154, art 7 at 1822.

17 MPC 213.1(1)(b).

18 Aquinas, *Theologica*, Benziger Q 154, art 7 at 1822.

19 MPC 213.1(1).

20 MPC 213.0(2).

21 Aquinas, *Theologica*, Benziger Q 154, art. 11-12 at 1825.

22 United States Supreme Court No. 02-102. Argued March 26, 2003; decided June 26, 2003.

23 Aquinas, *Theologica*, Benziger Q 154, art 12.

24 Aquinas, *Theologica*, Benziger Q 154, art 11.

25 Aquinas, *Theologica*, Benziger Q 154, art 11.

26 Aquinas, *Theologica*, Benziger Q 154, art 12 at page 1825.

27 Aquinas, *Theologica*, Benziger Q 154 ,art 12 at 1826.

28 Aquinas, *Theologica*, Benziger Q 154, art 12 at 1826.

29 Mass. Ann. Laws ch. 272, §§ 34, 35 (Law. Co-op. 1992). Section 34 proscribes sodomy and buggery, § 35 proscribes "unnatural and lascivious acts." *See* other jurisdictions such as: Mich. Comp. Laws Ann. § 750.158 (West 1991). In 1990, a Wayne County trial court invalidated the statute on privacy grounds in a suit brought against the county prosecutor and state attorney general; to date, neither defendant has appealed. See Frank Bruni, "Sodomy Statute is Struck Down: Laws Violate Right to Privacy, Judge Says," *Detroit Free Press*, July 10, 1990, at B1. Minn. Stat. Ann. §609.293 (West 1987). Miss. Code Ann. §97-29-59 (1999). This statute was recently

challenged unsuccessfully. *See* Miller v. State, 636 So. 2d 391 (Miss. 1994) (declining to reach the issue whether sodomy statute infringes state constitutional guarantee of privacy). 129 N.C. Gen. Stat. §14-177 (1999); S.C. Code Ann. §16-15-120 (Law. Co-op. 1985); 131 Utah Code Ann. §76-5-403(1) (1999).

30 United States Supreme Court No. 02-102. Argued March 26, 2003; decided June 26, 2003.

31 United States Supreme Court No. 02-102. Argued March 26, 2003; decided June 26, 2003, at Dissent #1.

32 Aquinas, *Theologica*, Benziger Q 154, art 12 at 1826.

33 Aquinas, *Theologica*, Benziger Q 154, art 12 at 1826 quoting *Confessions*.

34 Aquinas, *Theologica*, Benziger at Q 154, art 10 at 1824.

35 Aquinas, *Theologica*, Benziger at Q 154, art 10 at 1824.

36 Aquinas, *Theologica*, Benziger at Q 154, art 10 at 1824.

37 Aquinas, *Theologica*, Benziger at Q 154, art 10 at 1824.

38 Aquinas, *Theologica*, Benziger at Q 154, art 10 at 1824.

39 Aquinas, *Theologica*, Benziger at Q 154, art 10 at 1824.

40 Aquinas, *Theologica*, Benziger at Q 154, art 11 at 1825.

41 Aquinas, *Theologica*, Benziger at Q 154, art 12.

42 *Genesis* 37: 2.

43 Stuart Banner, *The Death Penalty: An American History* (London: Routledge: Taylor and Francis Group, 2002).

44 Aquinas, *Theologica*, Benziger Q 154, art 8 at 1822.

45 Aquinas, *Theologica*, Benziger Q 154, art 8 at 1822.

46 Aquinas, *Theologica*, Benziger Q 154, art 8 at 1822.

47 Aquinas, *Theologica*, Benziger Q 154, art 8 at 1822.

48 Aquinas, *Theologica*, Benziger Q 154, art 2 at 1816.

49 The American Enterprise Institute has tracked the rates for 4 decades. See http://www.aei.org/publications/pubID.18864/pub_detail.asp.

50 Aquinas, *Theologica*, Benziger Q 154, art 2 at 1816.

51 Aquinas, *Theologica*, Benziger Q 154, art 3 at 1818.

52 Aquinas, *Theologica*, Benziger Q 154, art 3 at 1818.

53 Aquinas, *Theologica*, Benziger Q 154, art 2 at 1817.

54 Aquinas, *Theologica*, Benziger Q 154, art 2 at 1816.

55 Aquinas, *Theologica*, Benziger Q 154, art 2 at 1816.

56 Aquinas, *Theologica*, Benziger Q 154, art 2 at 1816.

57 Aquinas, *Theologica*, Benziger Q 44, art 1 at 2722–2723.

68 Aquinas, *Theologica*, Benziger Q 44, art 3 at 2724.

59 Aquinas, *Theologica*, Benziger Q 66, art 1 at 2814.

60 Aquinas, *Theologica*, Benziger Q 66, art 1 at 2814.

61 Aquinas, *Theologica*, Benziger Q 66, art 1 at 2814.

62 Aquinas, *Theologica*, Benziger Q 66, art 1 at 2814.
63 Aquinas, *Theologica*, Benziger Q 66, art 2 at 2819.
64 Aquinas, *Theologica*, Benziger Q 66, art 2 at 2819.
65 Aquinas, Theologica, Benziger Q 65 art 1 at 2807.
66 John F. Dedek, "Intrinsically Evil Acts: An Historical Study of the Mind of St. Thomas," 43 *The Thomist* 392.
67 Aquinas, *Theologica*, Benziger Q 65, art 1 at 2808.
68 Aquinas, *Theologica*, Benziger Q 65, art 1 at 2808.
69 Aquinas, *Theologica*, Benziger Q 65, art 1 at 2809.
70 Aquinas, *Theologica*, Benziger Q 65, art 3 at 2811.
71 Aquinas, *Theologica*, Benziger Q 65, art 3 at 2811.
72 Aquinas, *Theologica*, Benziger Q 65, art 4 at 2812.

Chapter 5

Aquinas on Property Offenses

Introduction

WHEN CONSIDERING CRIMES INVOLVING PROPERTY, AQUINAS ARGUES LIKE a passionate Aristotelian. For St. Thomas the question of ownership was inexorably bound up in the idea of what is "due" or owing to another. To be sure, Aristotle's simplistic, though perfect definition of justice – giving to each and everyone what is due – sums up the rationalization for why property offenses rank so seriously in the Thomistic criminal code. It is not just ownership at stake, but what a person is worth, what they own and have worked for, and what these victims suffer so obviously – a lack of material and personal equilibrium after the victimization. Anyone who has ever been victimized by the thief or the robber intensely knows that feeling of emptiness, of invasion and attack in one's sphere of influence. Thievery and robbery do not find escape in St. Thomas' view as petty or common. Instead, he sees these acts as confrontations of the individual and the community in which the victim resides.

From his biblical exhortation that "Thou Shalt Not Steal" to his advanced view of private ownership and its corresponding rights and obligations, St. Thomas makes plain that property offenses are "in opposition to justice."[1]

The Right to Property

In his usual systematic way, St. Thomas lays out the nature of property before defining criminal acts against these forms of ownership. From the outset, the idea of private ownership by individuals is not a concept to be taken for granted. Whether in utopian designs, collective or socially stratified, royal or militaristic cultures, Aquinas sheds some extraordinary light on how an individual can actually own things. Property, some have argued, can only be described as communal. Others have offered the suggestion that property can only be truly or actually owned by God, since God is the Creator. Still others have argued that only the elites, the intelligentsia and their ilk, are really capable of property ownership. Everyone else resides in the servile class. St. Thomas accepts none of these conceptions but appears naturally comfortable with the democratization of property. The implications of this liberality will surely make a mark on the level and sophistication of his criminal-law theory.

In the Thomist worldview it can only be "natural" for the human person to own possessions. To the advocate who espouses that God owns the store, Aquinas urges a gaze at how human beings carry out existence. If God did not delegate the external things of the earth, why does the human person have some control of over them? The term "dominion" is often used to describe this form of human stewardship over the external things of earthly life. Aquinas remarks: "God has sovereign dominion over all things: and he, according to His providence, directed certain things to the sustenance of man's body. For this reason, man has a natural dominion over things, as regards the power to make use of them."[2] As man engages the temporal domain, he or she must exercise control not only over its natural functions and operations, but the particulars of human life – the growing of crops, the construction of a domicile, the payment of wages, and the protection of family. Aquinas refers to this commercial obligation as a sort of "managing and disposing" function.[3] To exist in any rational sense, human beings must catalog property, divide and sever its value, and apportion or ration according to need or merit. This cannot simply be accomplished as if in an idyllic utopia because human beings have an uncanny way of disappointing the idealists. Instead, Aquinas recognizes that human functionality mandates ownership of various things. As rational creatures, the human person will naturally take control of not only things but also human affairs in general. We are not a people of inaction. We are, as Aquinas holds, stronger and brighter than the comparative life forms we reside with. As though closer to perfect than the rest of the animal kingdom, the human person takes advantage of the less-perfect species and inanimate objects of living, as the "imperfect is always for the sake of the perfect."[4] We do, just as Scripture indicates that man is to have "dominion over the fishes of the sea."[5]

Hence to thwart this design by taking what another owns lawfully, and to be certain, very naturally, confronts the plan of creation. Property offenses strike at the very heart of why human beings need things in the first place. To survive and live, the human agent will acquire and use necessary forms of property. Indeed Aquinas argues that property ownership is consistent with his natural-law principles. In sum, how else can men and women live? Without ownership? With only commonly held valuations? Human affairs are complicated enough without the orderly transfer and identification of property forms. Imagine a culture where no ownership was ascribed to an individual. In its place, the citizens simply held that all that could be labeled was owned by the collective. For Aquinas it would be ludicrous to adopt this view of ownership, and without question, he held that this form of collectivism runs contrary to the human condition, and man must be "taking care of some particular things himself" which if not concerned about his self-preservation would otherwise be sown in a world of "confusion."[6]

St. Thomas offers up even more cogent reasons for the sanctity of property ownership and why it should not only be advanced but protected by criminal codifications. Without clear lines and distinctions of ownership, commerce becomes futile. Without a free system of property alienation, how can property be passed down or preserved for future generations? And in the absence of some formal system of property rights, how will citizens divide and apportion what has value? At the center of his commentary resides an insightful critique on why cultures that collectivize are communities bound to fail – why human nature, especially when lacking order and systematic processes, descends into a chaotic state. Aquinas rightly believes that without private ownership and the corresponding protections for property owners a culture will be rooted in chaos. He remarks that the "peaceful state is ensured to man if each is concerned with his own. Hence it is observed that quarrels arise more frequently where there is no division of the things possessed."[7]

Stalin and Chairman Mao prove the point – that collectivization, communism, and the socialist definition in the arena of property rights are the predictable sowers of turmoil in human affairs. In the end, property ownership manifests what is natural to the human condition and by most measures that which is conducive to growth and personal development. Property comports with the natural law since ownership is an "institution supplementary to the natural law and invented by human reason."[8]

For these and other reasons, Thomas gives significant care and attention to the role of property crime and the common good.

Theft and Stealing

Just as current codifications in the law of crimes do, Aquinas discerns theft in multivariate ways. While it is clear that the "taking" without right or privilege cannot be justified, St. Thomas dissects the act with many nuances. First, ownership of a thing implies certain rights that are attached to said property. While the illegal theft is an assault on the property itself, it is more aptly described as an attack on the person who has a possessory interest. Thomas keenly realizes that theft and robbery undercut and destroy the equilibrium that justice demands. The taking causes "what is due" to become a vacant ambition. Theft and robbery, like all other forms of crime, corrode the public order since the measure of justice can only be in restoration and the return of the equilibrium.

The "Taking"

As in modern codes, the thief must act. He may intend, but the act must correspond and be generated by intent. Thus, one can dream of thievery without restriction and culpability will never emerge. Theft constitutes a "taking," a separation of the object from the owner. Aquinas assumed that the mind of man alone would not reach the requisite level of action to be charged with crimes. St. Thomas delineates: "The first belongs to theft as being contrary to justice, which gives each one what is due, so it belongs to theft to take possession of what is another's."[9]

This "taking" explicitly connotes an unjust separation of a thing from the rightful owner. "Takings" that lack a possessory assault on the rights of another will not constitute theft. For example, one cannot steal from oneself since the possessory interest is self-evident. Neither can one steal an item that is abandoned or completely and utterly lost, since there is no figure who may or can make claim to a higher right to the property in question. Of course these latter cases are guided by notice and holding periods with lawful authorities. Even so, St. Thomas always zeroes in on the essence of the "taking" – understanding completely that the victim has been thrust into a collapsing equilibrium. It is theft because the victim "loses" something. It is theft because the only way to restore that loss is compensation or restitution. Modern sentencing models promote remedies for victims that are uncannily Thomist in design. Theories of restoration, restorative justice, restitution, and community service all recognize that until the victim is made whole, justice suffers.

From another angle, the "taking" is described as utterly "involuntary." Property owners who are sane do not wish for separation and theft. Theft, by its fundamental nature, can only be characterized as an involuntary act against the interest of another. Theft's taking is neither wished nor willed by its victim but is more accurately "suffered." Theft is "involuntary on the part of the person from whom something is taken."[10] For Thomas, the "taking" is an act of "violence" against that victim since there is no cooperation. In general, "takings" are possible either by ignorance or violence.[11]

In the former case, ignorance, the liability of the accused will really be in doubt. In the later case, the actor takes without right or privilege, and takes knowing full well that the property is not his for the taking. The act, Aquinas argues, is criminal when it is knowing and fully voluntary. At its center, the perpetrator realizes that he or she is "seizing upon what is another's."[12] The crux of this criminal definition, as well as most others in the world of Aquinas, can be found in Aristotelian justice – that what is due represents what is just. Any assault on this formula leads to crime.

Theft and Secrecy

As in most modern codifications, acts of theft are rarely carried out openly and with cooperation from the victim. St. Thomas attaches great importance on the idea of secrecy. The stealth and cunning of the act, the guile and deception needed, launch the seemingly harmless property offense into another dimension. Throughout the writings of St. Thomas, a consistent, almost virulent condemnation of falsehood appears with regularity. No place is this more evident than in his discussion of lawyers and judges – whose primary vocational and professional aim should relate to truth.

For the lawyer, truth is fittingly attributed to every aspect of law and its practice. At various places in the *Summa Theologica*, Thomas treats the opposite of truth-telling, dwelling upon falsehood, cheating in buying and selling,[13] willful deceit in the transfer of goods and services,[14] overstatement and unconscionability in the value of a thing,[15] violation of vows,[16] oaths,[17] perjury,[18] and lying.[19] Lying and falsehood are opposed to truth, St. Thomas states, except in accidental cases. Lying, "*mendacium*," is neither the product of negligence or involuntariness, but a formal declaration of falsity in "opposition to the *mind*"[20] (*contra mentem*). A lie is contrary to charity, in confrontation with justice, and an inequity.[21] Dissimulation and hypocrisy are as vigorously condemned by St. Thomas. Words, the sum and substance of lies and falsehoods, represent one of many means to falsehood. Signs, acts, and deeds that are disingenuous encompass falsity:

> Accordingly just as it is contrary to truth to signify by words something different from that which is in one's mind, so also is it contrary to truth to employ signs of deeds or things to signify the contrary of what is in oneself, and this is what is properly denoted by dissimulation. Consequently dissimulation is properly a lie told by the signs of outward deeds. Now it matters not whether one lie in word or in any other way, as stated above. Wherefore, since every lie is a sin, as stated above, it follows that also all dissimulation is a sin.[22]

St. Thomas' legal system depends on hard evidence, not suspicion, rumor, and doubt.[23] Suspicion, for example, is nothing more than a "perversity of the affections"[24] which cannot lead to the type of legal truth necessary for acquittal or conviction. Dubious ideas should not control legal reasoning because lawyers "strive to make [judgments] in accord with things as they are."[25] Truth has a hardness to it, be it the truth of temporality or universality. Falsehood, deceit, and deception have no place in Thomas' legal system.

In many ways Thomas seems utterly disgusted by falsehood of any sort. Lies, calumny, guile, cunning, and fraud all receive significant treatment by Aquinas. Why does Aquinas so passionately discuss the severity of falsehood? For him, the representations of the person were a window into his or her soul. To lie was to betray the fundamental goodness of the human person and to use the intellect in ways the Creator never intended. In the world of St. Thomas, most believe that human beings are inclined or predisposed, almost propelled, to do what is right. Lying undermines this natural propensity and as a result is considered a far more serious offense than in contemporary ethics. Sadly, lying, cheating, and fraud have become nearly acceptable in a relativist culture. But for St. Thomas the cheat and the liar deserved no respect whatsoever. The thief's secrecy rests side-by-side with the liar. By "stealth" property is seized from another and "is unjustly detained. . . . In disregard of the due course of law."[26]

Thievery was labeled a "mortal sin" by St. Thomas since the act corrodes the rights of others, and causes a rupture in the common good. For the thief "injures his neighbor in his property; and if all men were to promiscuously steal, human society would be lost. Hence theft is a mortal sin, as being contrary to charity."[27]

Secrecy encompasses the very essence of what the liar and cheat are so adept at. Theft is for the most part a secret act. While the distinction may be too subtle, the victim of theft generally has no awareness that the stolen interest is being pilfered, while the victim of a robbery knows very intimately the reality of the loss. In the robbery, the taker takes by force and violence, while in a case of theft, the taking generally arises in secretive situations. St. Thomas displays a sophisticated understanding of this distinction when formally comparing theft and robbery.

The remote end of robbery and theft is the same. But this is not enough for the identity of species, because there are different proximate ends, since the robber wishes to take a thing by his own power, but the thief, by cunning.[28]

Despite this secretive edge in theft, St. Thomas recognizes that events, circumstances, and legal nuances will not always condemn the secretive taking. The secret is simply not enough. The secrecy must be coupled with a lack of right to the property in question. The taker must be devoid of any legal right or claim and lacking in defensible justification. St. Thomas, however, does appreciate circumstances where stealth and secrecy are proper acts – say for the property owner who wishes to reclaim what is rightfully his, or who takes back under a court order.

Aquinas argues that "it is no theft to take another's property either secretly or openly by order of a judge who has commanded him to do so, because it becomes his due by the very fact that it is adjudicated by him by the sentence of the court."[29]

Even though St. Thomas is keen to allow victims of property theft the right to reclaim by secret means, this suggestion does have limitations. St. Thomas fully realizes that a distraught owner may take desperate steps to recapture stolen property. Yet, these steps must be attentive to the rule of law and not engage in reclamation that strikes at "general justice" by "usurping judgment concerning his own property."[30]

This view represents one of the consistent themes in his jurisprudence – that public authority provides a system that maintains order over its private counterparts. Courts, sentencing schemes, and law enforcement are best left to public officials rather than the whims of the private citizen. Here St. Thomas shows no difference in this preference since victims are encouraged to process their claim or grievance in the publicly crafted system which assures the "order of justice."[31]

Theft and Gravity

All modern statutory construction defines theft according to various degrees based on the gravity and seriousness of the offense. In American criminal parlance, the question would be one of degree or type – Theft in the 1st Degree, or Theft as a Class A versus Class F misdemeanor. Thomas understands the gradational quality of theft and lays out various issues regarding it.

Value of Property

The question of valuation of the property is a crucial issue for statutory design. The nature of the theft charge will depend on a host of factors including type of property, amount and value, and the conduct of the accused. Gravity, in short depends on what something is worth – just like the distinctions "petty theft" and "grand theft larceny." The terms reflect valuation. In the latter instance, the value is statutorily defined – say $2,500.00 in value or more. Aquinas asks similar questions but with a theological bent. In response to whether theft is always and in all cases a mortal sin, Thomas manifests a keen legal mind. While surely agreeing that theft is always a sin – since to take another's property causes a person to be "clearly guilty of sin"[32] – his sense of proportion waivers at the descriptor "mortal." Interestingly, St. Thomas reserves that final resolution to "Divine judgment."[33] In select cases, Thomas shows no hesitancy in reaching this conclusion relating to gravity, since theft assaults charity and suffers the neighbor.

> Now charity consists principally in the love of God, and secondarily in the love of our neighbor, which is shown in our wishing and doing him well. But theft is a means of doing harm to our neighbors in his belongings.[34]

Therefore, theft without mitigation and deriving from a clear and unequivocal will and free choice constitutes a mortal sin. Accepting this general view, Thomas moves forward with an erudite examination of why some thefts are more serious than others. In the first instance, St. Thomas looks to the property itself. What is it worth? How much do people value it? Who is the victim and how much will they miss it? Does the theft cause major injury to the victim? A close reading of St. Thomas indicates a willingness to review cases by factual severity. With adroit common sense, Thomas labels some thefts as nothing more than "little matters."[35]

> Reason accounts as nothing that which is little: so that a man does consider himself injured in very little matters. . . . And if a person take such very little things, he may be proportionately excused from mortal sin.[36]

Hence the Thomistic method is comfortable differentiating offenses based on valuation.

On another front, St. Thomas looks to circumstances that prompt the theft. In particular, St. Thomas listens to the argument of necessitous circumstances – that the theft arises out of true need and survival. At his time, poverty was widespread and the theft of foodstuffs was a common offense. St. Thomas sees the thief in light of his or her circumstances and when hunger drives the act, the question of mortal sin fades fast. Like a seasoned defense attorney, Thomas weighs mitigation in criminal culpability. He holds: "This necessity diminishes or entirely removes the sin."[37] St. Thomas sees necessity in hunger or in the passion to care for children without sustenance, even urging a reclassification of property from individual to common. In other words, in cases of true necessity (e.g. starvation and hunger), property metamorphisizes into a communal character. St. Thomas relays: "In cases of need all things are common property, so there would seem to be no sin in taking another's property for need has made it common."[38]

Human laws, St. Thomas urges, lose the power of enforcement in cases of true necessity. Since self-preservation is one of the natural law's primordial principles, any human proscription which forbids the maintenance of self is a law that cannot oblige. Thomas describes necessity as the equalizer in the survivorship of the human person. Any law which punished acts brought about by true necessity is inconsistent with the natural law. Survival and self-preservation cannot be derogated by the application or enforcement of any human law. But the case advocated of necessity is not one of mere trifle. Necessity implies an urgency and seriousness of condition that excuses culpability. St. Thomas puts it well: "Nevertheless if the need is manifest and urgent, that it is evident that the present need be remedied by whatever means be at hand."[39] By considering the economic value of the property in question and by the mitigating factors that give rise to necessity, St. Thomas delivers a criminal codification on theft that metes out proper justice.

Robbery

Much of Thomas' discussion of theft directly applies to his analysis of robbery. Similar to theft, the act of robbery targets property as its ultimate end. Thus, similar lines of inquiry will be raised in reaching proof of the charge. First, what property was taken? Second, was the property taken under a claim or right? Was the property taken? Was the property of any value? Are there any defenses to the taking such as necessity? While these questions do not perfectly fit in the robbery context, the issues still must be raised for successful prosecution of the offense. However, robbery has an additional element in its definition, namely the use of force. Robbery is the taking of property of another, without claim or right, although the action of taking need be violent and forceful. St. Thomas masterfully lays out the additional elements.

> Robbery implies a certain violence and coercion employed in taking unjustly from a man which is his.
>   . . . If a private individual not having public authority takes another's property by violence, he acts unlawfully and commits a robbery, as burglars do.[40]

The comparison between robbery and theft is authored on more than one occasion by St. Thomas. His emphasis relates to the force and aggression of robbery's taking. On close inspection, the robber, instead of using deceit and secrecy, directly confronts the victim in robbery. This awareness on the part of the victim is similar to the modern apprehension or imminent fear elements in some robbery statutes. It is difficult to convict on a charge of robbery when the victim had no awareness of the events leading to the loss of property. For violence to have its effect, the victim must realize the nature of the assault. Aquinas labels the robbery victim as less willing than his theft counterpart. The violence is a direct attack on the freedom of the human person and, as a result, causes greater harm to the victim. The phrase Thomas uses is "will than ignorance."[41] Finally, St. Thomas paints robbery as a crime of dual consequence and harm. While theft is primarily an offense against rightful ownership, robbery, by its imposition of force and violence does much more to the person victimized. Robbery consists of two harms: a "loss inflicted on another in his property, but there is also something of personal insult or injury enacted."[42]

Fraud

St. Thomas provides a very advanced look at property offenses involving consumers and commercial practice. Long before modern consumer advocates proclaimed remedies for fraudulent practices of business and individuals, Aquinas already set out a series of offenses that can be best set under the heading of fraud. At its heart, fraud is a property offense. And while it may lack the violence of robbery or the cunning and secrecy of theft, the harm that fraud causes to individuals and commercial institutions can only be described as extensive. Before the Consumer Protection Agency, before the Fair Credit Reporting Act, and before Lemon Laws, St. Thomas had already discovered that justice demands fairness in dealing and that the law of reciprocity could not be maintained in a corrupt exchange.

Fraud in the Price

At the foundation of his principles of commercial justice is Aristotle's law of equality and equilibrium, where goods and values have some connection, where buyers and sellers know and expect to get what one pays for. What is due is what a thing is worth – nothing more and really nothing less. St. Thomas, like Aristotle, would probably be unnerved by unrestrained capitalism and the materialism of excess. What is due can only be derived from contribution and worth, as well as value and uniqueness of the work. A journey into the world of St. Thomas will divulge a commercial philosophy based on justice. Anything else will come under the scrutiny of the suspected fraud.

What St. Thomas is searching for is equality in the bargain – that buyers get a product of value in exchange for consideration to a seller that is fair and equitable. There are two ways this can be measured. First, the use-value, which simply indicates what it costs to make. So if a television costs $500.00 – that is the price to charge. At first glance, this appears to be the approach taken by Aquinas. But on closer reading, St. Thomas is pushing a "market value" approach. What the market bears may be either more or even less than the use value. St. Thomas recognizes that market forces do dictate market practices by noting that "the just price of things is not fixed with mathematical precision."[43] St. Thomas will look to a theory of mutual advantage. If buyers are willing to pay a premium, and sellers wish the bargain, fraud would not be likely. St. Thomas fully understands market reality when he notes: "On the other hand if a man finds that he derives great advantage from something he has bought, he may, of his own accord, pay the seller over and above: and this pertains to honesty."[44]

Fraud and Commercial Practice

This same ideology as previously discussed applies to the skilled professional, the trader and the business person. Those skilled in trading, St. Thomas argues, are "commendable" when providing goods and services for the common good.[45] A safe and flourishing community relies on the goods and services of the trading class. Curiously, Thomas exhibits some nervousness about the vocation of the commercial trader, claiming that the temptation of the business can lead to debasement and obsession with materialism.[46] Briefly, Thomas expects the trader to make a living but only one necessary for stability and maintenance. Chasing the money, so to speak, above and beyond the basic necessities of life, leads to a sort of debasement. His language is quite fascinating and very telling when one weighs the current plague of materialism.

> Thus, for instance, a man may intend a moderate gain which he seeks to acquire by trading for the upkeep of his household, or for the assistance of the needy: or again, a man may take to trade for some public advantage, for instance, lest his country lack the necessaries of life . . .[47]

Anything more tests the virtue/vice continuum for the temptation for goods, the passions generated by greed, the corruptions of having too much, etc., and makes Thomas nervous about unbridled capitalism, and just as nervous about the potential for criminal conduct.

Trading, Thomas argues, is about worldly affairs and worldly gains and, without question, "open to so many vices."[48]

Much of what we read about contemporary business, excessive levels of compensation for corporate executives, athletes, scandals and betrayals of fiduciary loyalty, all attest to a market that may not lack efficiency but clearly lacks a conscience. St. Thomas would be distressed about the lack of virtue in so much of 21st-century commerce.

Fraud in the Exchange

At the base level, sellers and buyers are expected to be fundamentally honest about an exchange. Whether a car or a house, the seller should divulge any defects he or she knows that are present in the product. So too should the company, the estate, or other seller of goods and services. Failure to do so will prompt a wide array of civil and criminal remedies and actions at the state, local, and even federal level. St. Thomas provides some significant jurisprudence in this area.

Defects in the Exchange

When a representation about a product is made, the seller should be sure of its accuracy. In commercial practice, the description of the good or service to be sold must be accurate. Do otherwise and the seller runs the risk of a fraud allegation. Defects come in three forms in the world of St. Thomas. First, the product may suffer a quantity problem – the product is not the size or weight alleged, or the amount sold may be insufficient. Second, the quality may be suspect such as a lower grade than claimed, a less healthy animal, or questionable foodstuff. Finally, the item may in fact not be the item alleged at all. For example zirconium for diamonds, brass for gold, or other dilution of once acceptable material. Thomas calls any mixing "defective in its substance."[49]

In each of these cases, which may or may not be factually true, the finder of fact must look to the intentionality of the accused. What does the seller know? Is the seller aware of any past defective history? Are there facts or other suspicious information which would have led a reasonable seller to know of an existing defect? Is the seller acting in good faith and did they in fact lack formal knowledge of the defect? In the former case, St. Thomas calls the exchange fraudulent. Calling these types of exchanges "illicit" and "unjust materially,"[50] St. Thomas demands not only a declaration of fraud but also an order of restitution to bring equilibrium back to the players. This mandate is equally applicable to a buyer who unjustly benefits from a mistake in the bargain. St. Thomas relays:

> Moreover what has been said of the seller applies equally to the buyer. For sometimes it happens that the seller thinks his goods to be specifically of lower value, as when a man buys of copper, and then if the buyer be aware of this, he buys it unjustly and is bound to restitution.[51] Each case of fraud burrows into the mind of the seller and the buyer. When the parties engage in conduct that provides unjust enrichment or advantage, the fraud case sticks. When the action is borne of innocence, the level of culpability substantially reduces. Restitution would likely be a common remedy in all types of cases.

One other factor must be assessed before a finding of fraud – the materiality of the defect. For St. Thomas, there was a continual obligation for fair and just dealing with others. An Aristotelian at heart, Thomas called upon the parties to discern whether non-disclosure of a known defect was a basis for fraudulent conveyance. In the most general terms, the answer is yes. Latent, inherent, difficult-to-discover defects cause the most problems if they are major. Here one witnesses a reliant buyer being sold goods from a good-faith seller. If the defect is minor and incidental to the transaction the historic legal maxim of *caveat emptor* will pertain. For most Western jurisprudence, that maxim even applied in non-incidental cases, since the burden to discover the defects was laid upon the buyer. In the age of consumer protection that burden has largely evaporated. From the Thomistic perspective, materiality of the defect is an essential criterion for judicial intervention. Thomas lists two material examples that forge a type of strict liability on the part of the seller, namely "danger and loss."[52] If the seller knows that the transaction will cause loss or danger to the buyer, that constitutes an "unlawful and treacherous bargain," and the seller must remedy.[53] In material defects, the bargain rests on rotted footing that can be repaired only by major reconstruction and restoration. The goods are simply too defective to sustain the bargain. As Thomas describes:

> If a man sells a lame for a fleet horse, a tottering house for a safe one, rotten or poisonous food for the wholesome. Wherefore if such like defects be hidden, and the seller does not make them known, the sale will be illicit and fraudulent, and the seller will be bound to compensation for the loss incurred.[54]

On the other hand, if the flaw is blatantly obvious to the buyer, easily discoverable upon even a lame inspection, the seller is free from any further obligation. As Thomas humorously puts it: "But if the flaw is manifest, as when a horse has got only one eye. . .then he is not bound to declare the flaw. . ."[55] Citing Aristotle, St. Thomas expects some due diligence from the individual and commercial agents out buying and selling, for a "man judges of what he knows."[56]

When the conditions are "manifest,"[57] the remedies are radically different. When the conditions are hidden, and intentionally so, liability, both criminal and civil in design, attaches.

Summary

St. Thomas' insights into property ownership and rights are quite fascinating. He appears to be attuned to the frustration of collective and communal ownership and shows no signs of utopian naïveté. For those who argue that property cannot be owned except by all, St. Thomas resolutely points out the inevitability of this ideology. St. Thomas, for the most part, acts like a free marketeer. Given this, he places a more serious purpose on property crime than those who might hold otherwise. His analysis of theft and robbery anticipate all the elements posed in the Model Penal Code. His zeal for consumer protection in matters of fraud and commercial practice just as convincingly prove his concern for individuals at the mercy of an unregulated marketplace. Price, latent defects, and misrepresentation are succinctly covered by the Angelic Doctor.

Endnotes

1   St. Thomas Aquinas, *The Summa Theologica*, trans. Fathers of the English Dominican Province (New York: Benziger Brothers, Inc., 1947) II-II Q 66, art 6 at 1479.
2   Aquinas, *Theologica*, Benziger, Q 55, art 1 at 1476.
3   Joseph Rickaby, s.j., *Aquinas Ethicus: The Moral Teaching of St. Thomas 53–54* (London: Burns and Oates, Ltd., 1892) citing *Summa Theologica* II-II Q 66, art 2.
4   Aquinas, *Theologica*, Benziger Q 66, art 1.
5   *Genesis* 1:26
6   Aquinas, *Theologica*, Benziger Q 66, art 2.
7   Aquinas, *Theologica*, Benziger Q 66, art 2.
8   Rickaby at 55 citing *Summa Theologica* II-II Q 66, art 2.
9   Aquinas, *Theologica*, Benziger Q 66, art 3 at 1478
10 Aquinas, *Theologica*, Benziger Q 66, art 4 at 1478.
11 Aquinas, *Theologica*, Benziger Q 66, art 4 at 1478.
12 Rickaby at 55 citing *Summa Theologica* II-II Q 66, art 3.
13 Aquinas, *Theologica*, II, Benziger, II-II, Q 77.

14   Aquinas, *Theologica*, II, Benziger, II-II, Q 77, art 3.
15   Aquinas, *Theologica*, II, Benziger, II-II, Q 77, art 4.
16   Aquinas, *Theologica*, II, Benziger, II-II, Q 88, art 6.
17   Aquinas, *Theologica*, II, Benziger, II-II, Q 89.
18   Aquinas, *Theologica*, II, Benziger, II-II, Q 98.
19   Aquinas, *Theologica*, II, Benziger, II-II, Q 110.
20   Aquinas, *Theologica*, II, Benziger, II-II, Q 110, art 1, c.
21   Aquinas, *Theologica*, II, Benziger, II-II, Q 110, art 4.
22   Aquinas, *Theologica*, II, Benziger, II-II, Q 111, art 1, c. *Ita etiam opponitur veritati quod aliquis per aliqua signa factorum vel rerum aliquid significet contrarium ejus quod in eo est, quod proprie simulatio dicitur. Unde simulatio proprie est mendacium quoddam in exteriorum signis factorum consistens. Non refert autem utrum aliquis mentiatur verbo, vel quocumque alio facto, ut supra habitum est. Unde cum omne mendacium sit peccatum, ut supra dictum est, consequens est etiam quod omnis simulatio est peccatum.*
23   Aquinas, *Theologica*, II, Benziger, II-II, Q 60, art 3.
24   Aquinas, *Theologica*, II, Benziger, II-II, Q 60, art 3, c.
25   Aquinas, *Theologica*, II, Benziger, II-II, Q 60, art 4, ad. 2.
26   Aquinas, *Theologica*, II, Benziger, II-II, Q 66, art 5 at 56.
27   Aquinas, *Theologica*, II, Benziger, II-II, Q 66, art 6 at 56.
28   Aquinas, *Theologica*, II, Benziger, II-II, Q 66, art 4 at page 1479.
29   Aquinas, *Theologica*, II, Benziger, II-II, Q 66, art 5 at 1479.
30   Aquinas, *Theologica*, II, Benziger, II-II, Q 66, art 5 at 1479.
31   Aquinas, *Theologica*, II, Benziger, II-II, Q 66, art 5 at 1479.
32   Aquinas, *Theologica*, II, Benziger, II-II, Q 66, art 5 at 1479.
33   Aquinas, *Theologica*, II, Benziger, II-II, Q 66, art 5 at 1480.
34   Aquinas, *Theologica*, II, Benziger, II-II, Q 66, art 7 at 1479.
35   Aquinas, *Theologica*, II, Benziger, II-II, Q 66, art 6 at 1480.
36   Aquinas, *Theologica*, II, Benziger, II-II, Q 66, art 6 at 1480.
37   Aquinas, *Theologica*, II, Benziger, II-II, Q 66, art 6 at 1480.
38   Aquinas, *Theologica*, II, Benziger, II-II, Q 66, art 7 at 1480.
39   Aquinas, *Theologica*, II, Benziger, II-II, Q 66, art 7 at 1481.
40   Aquinas, *Theologica*, II, Benziger, II-II, Q 66, art 8 at 1480.
41   Aquinas, *Theologica*, II, Benziger, II-II, Q 66, art 9 at 1480.
42   Aquinas, *Theologica*, II, Benziger, II-II, Q 66, art 9 at 1480.
43   Aquinas, *Theologica*, II, Benziger, II-II, Q 77, art 1 at 1514.
44   Aquinas, *Theologica*, II, Benziger, II-II, Q 77, art 1 at 1514.
45   Aquinas, *Theologica*, II, Benziger, II-II, Q 77, art 4 at 1517.
46   Aquinas, *Theologica*, II, Benziger, II-II, Q 77, art 4 at 1517.
47   Aquinas, *Theologica*, II, Benziger, II-II, Q 77, art 4 at 1517.
48   Aquinas, *Theologica*, II, Benziger, II-II, Q 77, art 4 at 1517.

49 Aquinas, *Theologica*, II, Benziger, II-II, Q 77, art 2 at 1515.

50 Aquinas, *Theologica*, II, Benziger, II-II, Q 77, art 4 at 1517.

51 Aquinas, *Theologica*, II, Benziger, II-II, Q 77, art 4 at 1517.

52 Rickaby citing *Summa Theologica* II-II, Q 77, art 3.

53 Rickaby citing *Summa Theologica* II-II, Q 77, art 3.

54 Aquinas, *Theologica*, II, Benziger, II-II, Q 77, art 3 at 1516

55 Aquinas, *Theologica*, II, Benziger, II-II, Q 77, art 3 at 1516

56 Aquinas, *Theologica*, II, Benziger, II-II, Q 77, art 3 at 1516 citing *Ethics* at I 3.

57 Aquinas, *Theologica*, II, Benziger, II-II, Q 77, art 3 at 1516 citing *Ethics* at I 3.

Chapter 6
Offenses involving Judicial Process

Introduction

JUDICIAL PROCESSES, SUCH AS TRIALS AND WITNESS TESTIMONIES, TRIBU-
nals and hearings, adjudications of every sort, are guided by general virtue principles in the world of St. Thomas. Whether at court or
in the home, St. Thomas expects that the human player will display
virtue in all aspects of participation. He relates:

> The truth of life is the truth whereby a thing is true, not
> whereby a person says what its true. Life like anything else
> is said to be true, from the fact it attains its rule and meas-
> ure, namely, the divine law: since rectitude of life depends
> on the conformity to that law. This truth of rectitude is com-
> mon to every virtue.[1]

In general, St. Thomas detests the act of lying and reviles its legacy.
He expends considerable time discussing it and roundly condemns
it. "Thomas teaches that every lie is a sin, using the word 'sin' to
cover both venial and mortal. The reason is that words are naturally ordered to the manifestation of truth. Accordingly, to use words
to express the false is an abuse of nature . . ."[2] St. Thomas shows little hesitancy in the condemnation of falsehood: "But a lie is bad in
kind. For it is an act falling upon undue matter, for since spoken
words are naturally signs of thoughts, it is unnatural and undue
that someone signify by speech that which he does have in mind."[3]
In judicial processes the opportunities for truth and falsehood are
quite obvious, and St. Thomas is aware of how these falsehoods are
criminalized. Perjury, false accusation, judicial malfeasance, legal
malpractice and other impropriety, witness tampering, and evidentiary corruption are just a few examples of how, when, and where

the judicial process is subject to criminal contamination. St. Thomas precisely lays out the appropriate conduct of judges, lawyers, witnesses, and other participants in the judicial process. From the start, Thomas argues that "truth" governs all of it and any abandonment of truth is contrary to the definition of law. Truth is labeled by St. Thomas as a special virtue because to "say what is true is a good act; and virtue is that which makes its possessor good, and renders his action good."[4]

For St. Thomas, truth is simply inseparable from judicial operations, since without it, judicial process would be a sham. St. Thomas realizes that "legal" truth may sometimes be less than perfect as the problems of litigants and other parties are adjudicated. However, in an ideal sense, the legal system must always yearn for and crave truth in all things. The truth of the system's participants is what Aquinas is after – the judge who sentences, the lawyer who advocates, and the witness who gives testimony. It is "truth whereby a man, both in life and in speech, shows himself to be such as he is, and the things that concern him, not other, and neither greater nor less than they are."[5]

Proven from another perspective, St. Thomas uses the "lie" as evidence of truth's pre-eminent role in adjudication. "Lying's" Latin root – *mendacium* – signifies its conscious opposition to truth. St. Thomas gets to the heart of the problem: "And the intention of a bad will may bear on two things: one of which is that a falsehood may be told; while the other is the proper effect of the false statement, namely, that someone may be deceived."[6]

From every angle St. Thomas condemns the lie as in opposition to truth. Lies corrode and corrupt legal processes. For example, in a case of unjust accusation or malicious prosecution, the lie spreads its injury across a large field of victims. Each false accusation, St. Thomas argues, causes injury to the "person of the accused and against the commonwealth."[7] Each misrepresentation rots the collective as distrust flourishes and faith in our legal institutions crumbles bit by bit. As St. Thomas describes:

> Now a lie is evil in respect to its genus, since it is an action bearing on undue matter. For as words are naturally signs of intellectual acts, it is unnatural and undue for anyone to signify by words something that is not in his mind.[8]

St. Thomas also realizes that litigation is by no means a perfect exercise, and that advocacy and the delicacies of defense sometimes lead to shades of gray in the presentation. Thomas insists that the trier of fact or judicial officer take sufficient steps to corroborate testimony. He relays with his usual practical wisdom:

> For in human acts, on which judgments are passed and evidence required, it is impossible to have demonstrative certitude, because they are about things contingent and variable. Hence the certitude of probability suffices, such as may reach the truth in the greater number of cases, although it fall in the minority.[9]

In calling for multiple witness corroboration, by demanding that counsel advocate in factually legitimate claims, and in calling on jurists to heed the evidentiary deposit, St. Thomas posits truth as the guidepost for all legal processes.[10]

In every aspect of his overview on judicial processes, St. Thomas urges the participants to be forthcoming and honest in all deliberations. To act contrarily to this general heeding is to march down a path that "helps the ungodly. . . and deserves the wrath of the Lord."[11]

Lawyers and Truth

St. Thomas expends considerable time outlining the ethical conduct of lawyers. As an illustration, when should a lawyer advocate? What types of cases? What if the lawyer knows the case is based on falsehood or error? What if there is a total lack of merit? Here the demand for honesty and integrity is continuous. His coverage is equally comprehensive when it comes to judges and defendants alike. From whatever vantage point one gazes, St. Thomas expects the parties to advance truth and not obstruct justice as the processes unfold.

Central to any lawyer's vocation is truth. Legal advocates are cautioned that falsehoods are not only destructive to the justice system, but also to the soul. Acceptable legal advocacy can be tenacious, innovative, and creative, but not at the expense of justice and truth. Falsehoods of every sort are vociferously condemned by St. Thomas. Lawyers are not to be a party to any unjust law, for to advocate the merits of an unjust law is to advance injustice. Unjust laws bind neither lawyer nor client.

At trial or other legal proceeding, the lawyer needs to refrain from all falsehoods, suspicion, rumor, calumny, collusion, and evasion. Those who engage in such tactics should be barred from the practice of law. If the defense or prosecution is meritorious and factually grounded, Thomas insists the lawyer aggressively pursue it using the wits given to him by God. These general insights extend to witnesses, the presentation of evidence, and candor toward the tribunal. In sum, Thomas' portrait of a lawyer contains professional competencies, but more compellingly, a picture of the moral agent dedicated to virtue and truth, since to justice "is annexed truth."[12]

The Lawyer as Advocate

Delivering a legal argument, arguing for or against a particular law, precedent, or statute, urging the adoption of a specific principle in law or equity is the sum and substance of the advocate. Lawyers perform a myriad of functions, and throughout their professional careers will most assuredly include legal argument. It is the business of the advocate to vigorously represent a case or a client in their respective conditions and circumstances. Vigor of representation however, is not a license to act without moral parameters. *"Zealous representation,"* a *"vigorous defense," "unfailing loyalty to client and case,"* and being *"a hired gun"* for defense or prosecution are the standard "shop" descriptions for the lawyer/advocate. These depictions portray primarily a role, an occupation of touting or toeing the line or case argument and advocacy. Such bantering is an incomplete inquiry into the nature of advocacy since the advocate need delve into other underlying issues: 1) *the meritorious basis for claim or charge*; and, 2) *the justness and justice in the claim or charge.* In other words, the advocate, before tuning up the vocal chords, assesses the morality, the virtue, and the end result of the case to be advocated. Lawyers, in Thomas' moral setting, cringe at false factual averments and avoid any type of deliberate or selective ignorance of facts. Lawyers are in the business of justice, and Thomistic justice, as has been articulated before, is not the province of victories and legal scorecards. Adopting a tone of condemnation, Thomas chides the lawyer who advocates the *unjust cause*:[13] "It is unlawful to co-operate in an evil deed, by counseling, helping, or in any way consenting, because to counsel or assist an action is, in a way, to do it."[14]

For the lawyer, truth is fittingly attributed to every aspect of law and its practice. Falsehood implies an internal secrecy that is corrosive and corruptive to both lawyers and individuals since "secrecy is sometimes a cause of sin."[15] Falsehood in accusation, in any form, *calumny*, *collusion*, and *evasion*, are just as difficult for Thomas to tolerate, for each of the guiles "deceitfully hides"[16] the truth. Thomas actually screens candidates for admission into legal practice by assessing the candidate's character in relation to truth or falsity. Personal defects of the soul should be a basis for exclusion from the legal profession. Those already in the profession will be "debarred"[17] if found dishonest. "Persons of ill-repute, unbelievers, and those who have been convicted of grievous crimes"[18] are *unbecoming*[19] candidates for the lawyerly arts. Thomas' lawyer is the completely virtuous person who possesses the functional skills necessary to advocate legal claims, and "those who are defective in these points, are altogether debarred from being advocates either in their own or in another's cause."[20] Labeling certain falsehoods as "sins committed against justice,"[21] Thomas identifies various strategies in plaintiff and defense litigation, diverse approaches in the delivery of witness testimony, and the means adopted to save one's life or freedom. In each of these contexts, truth is the standard bearer and falsehood scathingly critiqued.

If truth drives the legal enterprise, then testimony gives life to its processes. When testimony is offered it is fair to assume that the truth will be told. Testimony is given under oath, and according to St. Thomas, an oath is a calling from God to bear witness to the content of the testimony. An oath is a serious undertaking, St. Thomas notes:

> From its origin, because the taking of an oath was brought in by the belief of mankind that God has infallible truth, possesses a universal knowledge, and exercises a universal providence over all things. From its end, because oaths are taken to justify men and put an end to disputes. . . . There is also danger of perjury because a man errs in his word.[22]

An oath signifies its dependency upon the Supreme Creator – because "God cannot lie, nor is anything hidden from him."[23] When giving testimony, a witness should remember the oath and give complete reverence to its purpose. The use of oaths assures greater credibility since when the "witness of God . . . is invoked, the man is bound to make true what he has sworn to, to the best of his power, unless the issues is for the worse."[24] Oaths promote truth since its end is "neither falsehood nor anything unlawful."[25]

Perjury

Perjury antagonizes truth and represents an intellect and will choosing to disregard truth. Perjury is an intentional act of falsehood, given under oath. St. Thomas calls perjury a major "deformity" – and a threefold deformity at that.[26] In the first sense, the deformity relates to falsehood under oath which confirms the conscious decision to lie. Secondly, the act of perjury has historically and universally been prohibited. Thomas labels perjury as an act antagonistic to the *jus*, that which is known to be true and right. On top of this he references the *Decalogue* about false witness against one's neighbor.[27] Third, perjury is always synonymous with the "lie," and lies are never anything but sin of some sort. From this assessment it is clear why St. Thomas holds perjury in such contempt. Aside from the corrosive impact on the judicial process, perjury manifests contempt for God and as result is "the most grievous"[28] of acts. St. Thomas holds: "To swear is to call God to witness. Now it is irreverence to God to call Him to witness to a falsehood, as though God either did not know the truth, or were willing to be a witness to what is false."[29] Perjury can only be classified as a "mortal sin" since "its own nature implies contempt of God."[30]

Malicious Prosecution

St. Thomas was keenly aware that a common abuse witnessed in the legal system related to malicious prosecution. Long a tool of intimidation, malicious prosecution consists of a filed legal action without a real or bona fide claim or remedy with the express purpose of using the legal system to harass and intimidate. Both the civil and criminal systems see their share of unfounded and ungrounded cases which are filed to antagonize and instill fear or to simply drain the resources of a targeted client. St. Thomas looks very closely at public authority and the role of a prosecutor in choosing to file actions or not. Just as pointedly, he looks to the private citizenry and its role in the initiation and prosecution of claims. While historically private claims posed by citizens were discretionarily filed, St. Thomas appears to argue that some types of cases are not discretionary but mandatory. On the hand, St. Thomas brooks no patience with a false filer of charge or claim. Thomas reserves the right of accusation to those cases that are not only injurious to the individual but the collective.

> Hence in the case of a crime that conduces to the injury of the commonwealth, a man is bound to accusation, provided he can offer sufficient proof, since it is the accuser's duty to prove: as for example, when anyone's sin condones to the bodily or spiritual corruption of the community.[31]

Petty, trivial cases, and unsubstantiated and doubtful cases will not compel action.

Aside from the issue of who may accuse and on what basis, the basis for any accusation must be sufficiently based in facts and law. If an accusation is based upon "calumny, collusion or evasion,"[32] it will be naturally suspect. By calumny, the accuser simply lies. By collusion, the accuser works with others to craft a false case, and finally by evasion whereby the accused subsequently withdraws without justification. In any of these cases, malicious prosecution exists because the motivation lacks a factual or legal basis and the intent is malicious. In short, the accuser who "falsely charges another with a crime is not a calumniator unless he give utterance to false accusations out of malice."[33] In cases of collusion, the parties work together deceitfully to create a false claim, such as an accused assaulter who colludes with the alleged victim for monetary gain. In collusion, the accused, "deceitfully hides the matter about which he makes the accusation."[34] In evasion, the withdrawal is caused not by a change of heart or facts, but some illegal benefit to withdraw from prosecution.

Each of these cases evinces falsehood and is contrary to Thomas' vision of legal truth.

The final element involving malicious prosecution is the right of wrongfully accused to bring forth a legal action for the unjustifiable process. While not mandatory, the law from Thomas' time to the present provides a remedy. In the absence of a clear-cut case, with no factual areas of dispute, and without proof of malice, the case will be difficult to prove. St. Thomas indicates the matter would be best left to judicial discretion by arguing: "All these things must be weighed according to the judge's prudence, lest he should declare a man to have been guilty of calumny, who through levity of mind or an error for which he is not to be blamed has uttered a false accusation."[35]

Thus cases of malicious prosecution should be evidentially strong and powerfully indicative of malice in the purpose. In the end, a successful prosecution of the charge establishes an equality of justice between them: and the quality of justice requires that a man should himself suffer what harm he causes.[36]

Judges and Truth

Any key role or position in the justice system envisioned by St. Thomas can only carry out its task and function when in accord with Thomas' overall philosophy. Judges are not only expected to pay more than glancing attention to the ideals of Thomistic jurisprudence, but to live and abide by its content. Judges short on justice and other virtues, or devoid of any teleological conception of law, will poorly perform the most basic of judicial functions, whether judgment, sentencing, evidentiary analysis, or testimonial evaluation. Judges, as ordinary men and women, are not another category of human species, but endowed like any other rational being. Thomas calls judging a "craft,"[37] indistinguishable from human identity.

At the forefront, judges serve as gatekeepers to judicial process and as arbiters of the dispute and disputants. Judges must be persons of virtue and integrity. St. Thomas disqualifies those unfit in soul or spiritual health from the judicial role or those "who stand guilty of grievous sins should not judge those who are guilty of the same or lesser sins."[38]

A judge deficient in moral or intellectual virtue is incapable of judging correctly. A judge failing to exercise right reason predictably will issue improper and incoherent rulings. An unjust judge not only lacks justice but all the other virtues necessary for the good life and acts not in accordance with the prescription for the moral life but contrary to its ends.[39] Thomas' judge labors not solely in a functional sense but in a holistic way – blending competency of task with competency of soul. A judge's "task is justice."[40] The perfectly good person is the perfectly good judge "subject to the overruling of providence as is all creation."[41]

At no place is the evidentiary genius of St. Thomas more apparent than in his discussion of evidence, truth, and the power of a judge[42] to rule. Here, Thomas integrates the role and occupation of a judge with that of the human person who dons the robes. Thomas vigorously corrects the advocate who thinks it possible for a judge to separate judicial decision-making from the evidence presented. Cases of whatever sort or kind can be decided on a host of rationales that are bankrupt of evidentiary rigor, replaced by sentimental, racist, political, criminally corrupted, mindless, or angry decision-making. Thomas scolds those who want justice without the evidentiary record to support it. In one case a judge, as a person, may know or feel something, none of which has been submitted by the advocates. In another, the formal record of evidence may be insubstantial and vacuous. How does the judge decide? It is the role as judicial information gatherer that provides the basis for judicial reasoning, not the private knowledge of the citizen who dons the robes. Judgment is "based on information acquired by him, not from his knowledge as a private individual, but from what he knows as a public person."[43]

If that same judge cannot pronounce evidentially, acquittal or dismissal is proper. So, Thomas suggests the real, indisputable truth may exist simultaneously with a legal truth, derived from either strong or weak evidence. In every case before the court, decisions have to be evidentially rooted. The judge may know after sifting through the evidentiary record that a decision soon to be rendered is contrary to the truth of the matter. Legal truth depends so heavily upon the court's evidentiary record that any judgment rendered will rest upon this legally suspect conclusion than the unsubstantiated, though true, allegation. For Thomas, the personal conscience of a judge is subject to the functionality of the judgeship. "In matters touching his own person, a man must form his conscience from his own knowledge, but in matters concerning the public authority, he must form his conscience in accordance with the knowledge attainable in the public judicial procedure."[44]

Defendants and Truth

How St. Thomas holds defendants accountable, when compared to contemporary visions of defense practice, could only be described as different in a draconian sense. In modern defense practice, the notion that a defendant has certain moral and spiritual obligations as to truth and falsehood seems almost laughable. But St. Thomas was dead serious when he insisted that the issues of criminal culpability and the salvation of one's soul were intimately intertwined. In other words, the Thomistic defendant does not detach the internal self from the external system about to adjudicate his circumstances. The Thomistic defendant cannot sever personal responsibility from the adjudication about to unfold. St. Thomas would not and could not understand a man who knows guilt, accepts it internally but then stands before the docket either silent or in denial. This is a lost soul for the ages in the jurisprudence of St. Thomas. Comparatively, modern legal practice could not envision this sort of interplay between legal innocence and the state of a person's true soul. While the defendant may not be compelled to admit guilt, if the order of due process leads to questioning by lawful superiors, the defendant, if truly guilty, needs to admit to that lawful authority or be in a state of mendacity. St. Thomas covers the point clearly.

> Therefore, the accused is duty bound to tell the judge the truth which the latter exacts from him according to the form of the law. Hence if he refuses to tell the truth which he is under obligation to tell, or if he mendaciously denies it, he sins mortally.[45]

On closer scrutiny there is a very fine line here. While St. Thomas has no true understanding of self-incrimination principles, he does not expect the prosecution to not carry out its task with professionalism. His greater concern is when the order of process allows for the questioning. Here the lie will be just as unacceptable as everywhere else in his legal philosophy. His commentary could not be clearer:

> He who lies in court by denying his guilt, acts both against the love of God to whom judgment belongs, and against the

}117{

love of his neighbor, and this not only as regards the judge, to whom he refuses his due, but also regards his accuser, who is punished if he fail to prove his accusation.46

St. Thomas has little patience for defendants who defend with lies, or by "calumnies."[47] It is one thing, he urges, not to divulge everything when under no compulsion to do so, but quite another to affirmatively engage in subterfuge and fraud. Defend oneself but do not do so with the corruption of the lie or by employing "guile or fraud because fraud and guile have the force of a lie.[48] The same reticence will apply to defendants who appeal without any right or justification. If a just sentence or other finding has been applied, and that finding is consistent with the truth, any appeal would be construed as a falsehood by St. Thomas. Appeals for purposes of delay, unfounded tactics, or other unjustified motives are labeled unlawful.[49] Even in a capital case, when death is imminent, the parameters of defense are not unlimited. Consistent with his other views of due process and adjudication, St. Thomas views the defendant as both temporal and metaphysical in design. What appears so often lost on the current millions presently incarcerated in prisons throughout the world is that life consists in two stages – the present and the eternal afterlife. St. Thomas views these defendants in a prism which includes both dimensions. A guilty man who continues to pursue appeals that he lucidly understands as contrary to the facts, sins. In this perspective we can appreciate how Thomas sums up the human species – as a being with a mind, body, and a soul. Efforts to deny the truthful reality which leads to a truthful responsibility are unacceptable legal tactics and obstructions of justice. For a man condemned justly should not resist the restoration of the equilibrium. St. Thomas crafts it as such: "Now a condemned man, by defending himself, resists the power in the point of its being ordained by God for the punishment of evil-doers, and the praise for the good. Therefore he sins in defending himself."[50] When evaluated in light of current legal practices, suggestions like these appear contrary to contemporary visions of right. Yet, if one dwells on it a little, the wisdom pours forth. Surely, our current correctional model fosters a complete lack of personal responsibility and even more distressingly an abandonment of all things spiritual. The sheer numbers of lost souls, who fail to accept personal responsibility for wrongs committed, is staggering. St. Thomas offers up another road to assuring freedom in the life to come.

It is a chance to live like the rational man God intended in his exemplar, to cast aside the slavish, brutish habits that dominate both intellect and will. If not, the eternity of the afterlife will not be in the ultimate end, the joy and wonder of the Beatific Vision of God, but the misery and agony of damnation. The criminal's most pressing loss is in being "cut off from happiness."[51] The assurance of salvation is the ultimate aim of restitution and any other method of punishment.[52]

Summary

That St. Thomas was obsessively preoccupied with matters of truth and that he was repulsed by falsehood is a most accurate description of his person. He expends considerable energy lashing out against those who lie in general, and he more pointedly condemns those in the legal system who engage in falsehood. The lie for St. Thomas has no quarter in judicial process. Truth, not falsehood, is what rests compatibly with the legal system. Hence, St. Thomas covers crimes such as perjury and malicious prosecution with fervent intellectualism. Perjury is contempt for God. Using the legal system under false or malicious circumstances is fiercely condemned by St. Thomas since it a spiritual corruption of not only the system but the community in which it resides.

The remainder of the chapter stresses particular occupations and roles in the legal system, namely, lawyer, judge, and defendant, and how crucial the role of truth is within all these roles. Falsehood cannot be tolerated whether it be case or claim, judicial decision or testimony itself.

Endnotes

1 St. Thomas Aquinas, *The Summa Theologica*, trans. Fathers of the English Dominican Province (New York: Benziger Brothers, Inc., 1947) II-II, Q 109, art 2 at 1662.

2 Lawrence Dewan, "St. Thomas, Lying and Venial Sin," *The Thomist*, 1997. 279–300.

3 Aquinas, *Theologica*, II, Benziger II-II, Q 110, art 1.
4 Aquinas, *Theologica*, II, Benziger II-II, Q 109, art 1 at 1661.
5 Aquinas, *Theologica*, II, Benziger II-II, Q 109, art 3 at 1663.
6 Aquinas, *Theologica*, II, Benziger II-II, Q 110, art 1 at 1664.
7 Aquinas, *Theologica*, II, Benziger II-II, Q 68 page 1489.
8 Aquinas, *Theologica*, II, Benziger II-II, Q 109, art 3 at 1666.
9 Aquinas, *Theologica*, II, Benziger II-II, Q 70, art 2 at 1498
10 Aquinas, *Theologica*, II, Benziger II-II, Q 71.
11 Aquinas, *Theologica*, II, Benziger II-II, Q 71, art 3 at 1498.
12 Aquinas, *Theologica*, II, Benziger, II-II, Q. 80, art 1, c.
13 Aquinas, *Theologica*, II, Benziger, II-II, Q 71, ar 3.
14 Aquinas, *Theologica*, II, Benziger, II-II, Q 71, art 3, c. *Quod illicitum est alicui cooperari ad malum faciendum, sive consulendo, sive adjuvando, sive qualitercumque consentiendo, quia consilians et coadjuvans quodammodo est faciens.*
15 Aquinas, *Theologica*, II, Benziger, II-II, Q 66, art 3, ad. 1.
16 Aquinas, *Theologica*, II, Benziger, II-II, Q 68, art 3, ad. 2.
17 Aquinas, *Theologica*, II, Benziger, II-II, Q 71, art 2, c.
18 Aquinas, *Theologica*, II, Benziger, II-II, Q 71, art 2, c.
19 Aquinas, *Theologica*, II, Benziger, II-II, Q 71, art 2, c.
20 Aquinas, *Theologica*, II, Benziger, II-II, Q 71, art 2, c. *qui in his defectum patiuntur, omnino prohibentur ne sint advocati nec pro se, nec pro aliis.*
21 Aquinas, *Theologica*, II, Benziger, II-II, Q 69.
22 Joseph Rickaby, S.J., *Aquinas Ethicus: The Moral Teaching of St. Thomas* (London: Burns and Oates, Ltd., 1892), 149, citing *Summa Theologica*, Q 89, art 3 at 149.
23 Rickaby at 148 citing *Summa Theologica* II-II, Q 89, art 3.
24 Rickaby at 152 citing *Summa Theologica*, II-II, Q 89, art 7.
25 Rickaby at 150 citing *Summa Theologica*, II-II, Q 89, art 4.
26 Aquinas, *Theologica*, II, Benziger, II-II, Q 70, art 4 at 1494.
27 Aquinas, *Theologica*, II, Benziger, II-II, Q 70, art 4 at 1494.
28 Aquinas, *Theologica*, II, Benziger, II-II, Q 70, art 4 at 1494.
29 Rickaby at 178 citing *Summa Theologica*, II-II, Q 109.
30 Rickaby at 179 citing *Summa Theologica*, II-II, Q 109 art 3.
31 Aquinas, *Theologica*, II, Benziger, II-II, Q 68, art 1 at 1486.
32 Aquinas, *Theologica*, II, Benziger, II-II, Q 68, art 3 at 1487
33 Aquinas, *Theologica*, II, Benziger, II-II, Q 68, art 3 at 1488.
34 Aquinas, *Theologica*, II, Benziger, II-II, Q 68, art 3 at 1488.
35 Rickaby at 66 citing *Summa Theologica* Q 68, art 3.
36 Aquinas, *Theologica*, II, Benziger, II-II, Q 68, art 4 at 1488.
37 Aquinas, *Theologica*, II, Benziger, II-II, Q. 57, art 1.

38 Aquinas, *Theologica*, II, Benziger, II-II, Q. 60, art 2, ad 3. *Quod illi qui sunt in gravibus peccatis, non debent judicare eos qui sunt in eisdem peccatis, vel minoribus.*

39 One of the few close looks at Thomistic jurisprudence in contemporary legal practice is Rev. Michael Harding, "True Justice in Courts of Law," in 3 Aquinas, *Theologica*, II, Benziger, II-II, 3348–49.

40 J. V. Dolan, "Natural Law and Judicial Function," *Laval Theologique et Philosophique* 16 (1960): 107.

41 E. Gilson, *Law on the Human Level: Moral Values and Moral life: The System of St. Thomas*, trans. L. Ward, C.S.C (St. Louis: B. Herder, 1931), 197.

42 Aquinas, *Theologica*, II, Benziger, II-II, Q. 67, art 2.

43 Aquinas, *Theologica*, II, Benziger, II-II, Q. 67, art 2, c. *et ideo informari debet in judicando non secundum id quod ipse novit tanquam privata persona, sed secundum id quod sibi innotescit tanquam personae publicae.*

44 Aquinas, *Theologica*, II, Benziger, II-II, Q. 67, art 2, ad 4. *Quod homo in his quae ad propriam personam pertinent, debet informare conscientiam suam ex propria scientia; sed in his, quae pertinent ad publicam potestatem, debet informare conscientiam suam secundum ea quae in publico judicio sciri possunt, etc.*

45 Aquinas, *Theologica*, II, Benziger, II-II, Q 69, art 2 at 1490.

46 Aquinas, *Theologica*, II, Benziger, II-II, Q 69, art 2 at 1490.

47 Aquinas, *Theologica*, II, Benziger, II-II, Q 69, art 2 at 1490.

48 Aquinas, *Theologica*, II, Benziger, II-II, Q 69, art 2 at 1491.

49 Aquinas, *Theologica*, II, Benziger, II-II, Q 69, art 3 at 1490.

50 Aquinas, *Theologica*, II, Benziger, II-II, Q 69, art 4 at 1492.

51 St. Thomas Aquinas, *Summa Contra Gentiles*, trans. Vernon Bourke, 2nd ed. (Garden City, N.Y.: Hanover House, 1956; Notre Dame, Ind.: University of Notre Dame Press, 1975) III-II, ch. 141, 3.

52 Aquinas, *Theologica*, II, Benziger II-II, Q. 62, art 2, c. *Cum ergo conservare justitiam sit de necessitate salutis, consequens est quod restituere id quod injuste ablatum est alicui, sit de necessitate salutis.*

Chapter 7

Aquinas on Offenses against Public Morality

Introduction

AS IN ALL CATEGORIES OF CRIMINAL LAW, ST. THOMAS OFFERS UP SUGGES-tions for the design and makeup of specific charges relating to public morality. In the broadest of contexts, public morality concerns itself with those actions that are injurious to the public in a behavioral sense. Compared to crimes against person and property, public-morality crimes tend to offend the sensibilities of the multitude and unsettle established communities. Just as the homeowner should not need to contend with drunks and drug addicts on his doorsteps, the park visitor should not be assaulted with public sexual acts, homeless behavior, and other disorderliness. Crimes against the public order are those generally involving the behaviors that offend the majority of the citizenry.

Public Drunkenness and Disorder

In one of his more curious and complicated discourses, St. Thomas evaluated drunkenness from a variety of perspectives. Drunkenness, in the most general sense, may be classified less as sinful and more instructively, a "defect" of sorts.[1] The defect relates to the party's mental functionality and distress in rational operations, and indicates incapacity to be in control or possess the necessary sobriety. Contrasted with sobriety, which "consists in the reasonable and temperate use of intoxicating drink,"[2] drunkenness represents an immoderation of behavior that cannot be legitimate. Drunkenness undermines the power of reason, and as a result, constitutes an error. St. Thomas relays:

> Drunkenness may be understood in two ways. First it may signify the defect itself of a man resulting from his drinking much, the consequence being that he loses the use of reason. In this sense, drunkenness is not a sin but a penal defect resulting from a fault. Secondly, drunkenness may denote the act by which a man incurs this defect.[3]

Thomas wisely observes that not all cases of drunkenness rise to the level of sin, though if this be true, the act may still lead to a finding of crime. Equally interesting is the point Thomas proffers relative to how one drinks for the moment, with a temporary defect in reason, but that same act can multiply over time to create the more permanent defect of reason. Anyone exposed to alcoholics soon learns that reasonable thinking about the vice quickly vanishes. Throughout his examination, St. Thomas displays a remarkable understanding on the role of alcohol in human and social life. St. Thomas is not a prohibitionist, but is better typified as one who assesses drink in light of circumstances. For example, St. Thomas refuses to answer affirmatively the query whether alcoholism is the "gravest of sins."[4] He seems to understand that this is the type of failing that commonly occurs in the human journey. He states:

> Man is most prone to sins of intemperance, because such like concupiscences and pleasures are connatural to us, and for this reason these sins are said to find greatest favor with the devil, not for being graver than other sins, but, because they occur more frequently among men.[5]

Even if we accept this practical observation about human history, that drinking appears inevitable, it would be foolhardy to think Thomas will not condemn the act. However, his intensity of condemnation will depend on the stage or evolution of alcohol in the life of the human agent. Paul Glenn summarizes:

> Drunkenness is a mortal sin in the person who willingly and knowingly deprives himself of the use of reason by excessive drinking. Reason is man's guide and control for the exercise of virtue and the avoiding of sin. Foolishly and

unwarrantedly to deprive oneself of reason is therefore a serious fault.[6]

Thomas erects a tri-tiered continuum of culpability in drunkenness as so:

> First, so that he knows not the drink to be immoderate and intoxicating; and then drunkenness may be without sin. . . . Secondly, so that he perceives the drink to be immoderate, but without knowing it be intoxicating, and then drunkenness may involve a venial sin. Thirdly, it may happen that a man is well aware that the drink is immoderate and intoxicating, and yet he would rather be drunk than abstain from drink. Such a man is a drunkard properly.[7]

In the last case, St. Thomas would surely impute criminal culpability since knowledge and intent to become drunk coalesce because "a man willingly and knowingly deprives himself of the use of reason."[8]

If the drinker has clear-cut knowledge, the act of drunkenness is not only a crime but a mortal sin. Further, this conclusion is buttressed by the willingness of St. Thomas to count and measure the multiplicity of acts that involve drunkenness. St. Thomas knows that the addiction to alcohol will foster repetition of the act. Referring to this as assiduous drinking, St. Thomas appears well aware of the power of alcohol to shape personalities and generate victims. He remarks: "It is impossible for a man to become drunk assiduously without exposing himself to drunkenness knowingly and willingly, since he has many times experienced the strength of wine and his own liability to drunkenness."[9] Like a modern alcohol and drug counselor, St. Thomas is attuned to the cumulative effects of drinking. Whether for the short or the long term, alcohol impacts the brain and its intellectual power. St. Thomas insists that drinking in excess harms the actor in two ways – both of which return to the increasing pathology surrounding reason and intellectual operations.

> The good of reason is hindered in two ways: in one way by that which is contrary to reason, in another by that which is contrary to reason has more the character of evil, than that which takes away the use of reason for a time, since the use of reason, which is taken away by drunkenness may be

either good or evil, whereas the goods of virtue, which are taken away by things that are contrary to reason, are always good.[10]

Hence, drunkenness manifests both qualities – as social problem, and alternatively, a criminal problem. Only when intent is matched with the act would criminal culpability attach.

Drunkenness and Mitigation

Few positions St. Thomas adopts can likely be described as liberal; if anything, readers are rarely surprised by St. Thomas, though his examination of drunkenness delivers some surprises. For example, we have already covered the first trimester analysis in abortion, and for doctrinaire pro-life advocates, it is somewhat unsettling when the Angelic Doctor suggests a contrary perspective. Such will be the case here too. St. Thomas allows for drunkenness to be a defense tactic in criminal prosecutions, and at a minimum, he thinks it wise to consider it as a form of mitigation. Modern criminal practice liberally employs a bevy of mitigating factors in the analysis of culpability. Addictions, passion and emotion, rage and anger, mental defect and disorder and a history of mental disease, to name a few, are frequently offered up as mitigators – quasi-explanations that either defend or reduce the severity of the charge. The list of mitigating factors is quite long. While many courts are reticent to accept drunkenness and drug addiction as a mitigator, and in some circles, like the Model Penal Code, these mitigators are expressly excluded in insanity defenses,[11] too often the addiction to alcohol is posited as some sort of health factor. It is common now to define drunkenness as a disease. St. Thomas seems quite at home with this type of defendant scrutiny and seems just as warm and fuzzy over the excuse that "alcohol made the party do it!" This is surprising for a thinker of his stature, and it is one of the few places he displays a softness in his judgment. In the *Summa Theologica* he even cites the story of Lot, in the Old Testament, whose drunkenness precipitates an act of incestuous sexual intercourse. In Lot's case, the drunkenness was not willed, and as a result, "if the drunkenness that results from that act be without sin, the subsequent sin is entirely excused from fault, as perhaps in the case of Lot."[12]

Contrarily, if the drunkenness were the latter variety, discussed above, then the subsequent act would be a crime. For lack of a better explanation, St. Thomas accepts that alcohol jumbles and blinds the actor, confuses and retards judgment. Alcohol, he argues, makes volition less likely, and voluntariness less pure.

Not only does Thomas mitigate crimes due to the influence of alcohol, he urges even less sin for this version of human offense. St. Thomas presents an extraordinary tolerance not often witnessed in his works, when he states: "Nevertheless, the resulting sin is diminished, even as the character of voluntariness is diminished."[13] While it is true that the criminal offender, who is intoxicated, may possess less than crystalline reason, adopting the posture of St. Thomas would have negative implications for victims, and by any prudential measure, would foster advanced drunkenness in those about to commit crimes. In this assessment, St. Thomas does not exhibit his usual prudential genius. One can only wonder what forces, in his life and circumstances, led to these conclusions.

Disorderly Conduct/Public Fighting

While St. Thomas does not expressly define disorderly conduct as crime, his coverage of human behavior, particularly as it relates to virtue and vice, envelops the issue from many fronts. Contemporary disorderly statutes are primarily concerned about public peace and tranquility and the maintenance of order among individuals and groups. Living with others in charity and respect is a tall order to fill. For St. Thomas, human interaction and personal interrelationships could often be filled with stress and discord. He is well aware of the fractures that occur in the social context and promulgates a series of prescriptive behaviors that advance charity in human relations.

Hatred and Human Interaction

The opposition to charity is formally rooted in hatred and dislike. It is hatred that often drives and prompts discord among people. From the most basic of commandments – to love one another – St. Thomas erects an array of errors that human fall into. In the most general sense, disorder arises from dislike and hatred of others, as St. Thomas states: "Hatred is opposed to love. . . . So that hatred of a thing is evil according as the love of that thing is good. Now love due to our neighbor in respect of what he holds from God, i.e., in respect of nature and grace. . . ."[14]

Though hatred may not be the most grievous of sins, St. Thomas appreciates its capacity to precipitate difficulties in human interaction. He labels hatred a grave evil that causes "disorder in the person" who hates and "hurt inflicted on the person sinned against."[15] Hatred provides the infrastructure for disorder and conduct unbecoming. Hatred, St. Thomas describes, "is a man's last step in the path of sin, because it is opposed to the love which he naturally has for his neighbor."[16]

Discord

All public contentiousness contains some quality or level of discord between people. Public disorder offenses presume that the wills of contrary parties are at war or in opposition. Whether driven by drink or lust, hatred or anger, public squabbles are often nothing more than a test of wills and egos. St. Thomas employs the term "discord" to describe this war of the wills, and the negative effects on human interaction. Discord implies a ruination of the "concord," the agreement among neighbors to live peacefully and respectfully with one another. St. Thomas puts the concept inside the interrelationships that human beings experience in communal life. "Wherefore a man directly disaccords with his neighbor, when he knowingly and intentionally dissents from the Divine good and his neighbor's good, to which he ought to consent."[17]

It is not difficult to imagine circumstances which corroborate this definition – neighbors fighting over property lines and fences, noise and other clamor without respect for themselves or others, and petty disputes and disagreements over minor issues. Every neighborhood has these sorts of characters whose primary reason for continued living rests in the antagonism that can be generated between the parties. This "disunion of wills" causes the community to suffer stress and a lack of cohesion. In short, discord is the byproduct of vainglory and envy, hatred and pride whereby "one man's will holds fast to one thing, while the other man's will holds fast to something else."[18] Discord brings even the "greatest to ruin."[19] Discord can be properly described as the "destruction of peace."[20]

Contention

When dealing with contention St. Thomas gives insight into the power of words rather than deeds. Words can be hurtful and do cause distress and disorder in communities. Contention "is discord that [finds] expression in words."[21] St. Thomas elaborates on the comparison: "Wherefore just as discord denotes a contrariety of wills, so contention signifies a contrariety of speech."[22] Contention also connotes holding to a position that cannot be defended, knowing the falsity of the position, yet still adhering to it. In this way, contention finds its impetus from envy and vainglory. Contention "is akin to envy" because the party contending is driven not by factual truth but another agenda.[23] Contentiousness often arises from excessive pride and a lack of true knowledge. If one ever argues with one ill-prepared, contentiousness frequently crops up because the argument is based on ignorance. To be frank, it is never easy to argue with or debate an ignorant person. Contention, based on defense of what is true and universal in design, such as established doctrine, can be defensible and even "praiseworthy."[24] In all other cases, contention will be adjudged based not only on the topic in contention, but also, the "manner of contending."[25] Thus, one may even be right in position and stance, yet how said position is argued may be less than charitable and as a result still contentious. Making a mountain out of a molehill, arguing with passion over a matter not worthy of the effort, constitutes a procedural contentiousness even though the substance of the argument may be legitimate. In this case, the argument "exceeds the demands of the persons and matter in dispute, in which case it is blameworthy."[26] In sum, St. Thomas asks us to be charitable and gentle in our debates and disagreements, to avoid the influence of pride in the argument and be more inclined to "humility."[27]

Strife

As contention involves words and argument, strife is about deeds and action. St. Thomas extends very little mercy to those engaged in strife – to those who assault each other in anger and argument. Those engaged in strife "shall not obtain the Kingdom of God."[28] Comparing strife to a battle, St. Thomas condemns the action.

"Hence strife is a kind of private war, because it takes place between private persons, being declared not by public authority, but rather by an inordinate will."[29]

Always ready to sow confusion, the strife agent operates with all the wrong motivations. To cause physical fights, to hit other people in anger, in hatred, and in envy, represents confrontation on two levels – to the individual and to the community at large. For St. Thomas, the agent who desires strife also desires vengeance, for "the angry man is not content to hurt secretly the object of his anger, he even wishes him to feel the hurt and know what he suffers is in revenge for what he has done."[30] Strife encompasses an "antagonism" to others by and through specific deeds. Strife nurtures ill will and discord and causes communal tension. St. Thomas accurately delineates the characteristic of the actor in strife.

> First, the quarrelsome man is always ready to fight, and this is conveyed by the words, "ever ready to contradict," that is to say, whether the other man says or does well or ill. Secondly, he delights in quarrelling itself, and so the passage proceeds, and "delights in brawling." Thirdly, he provokes others to quarrel, where it goes on, "and provokes contention."[31]

To our misfortune, this character description is all too often witnessed – outside bars and entertainment facilities, in neighborhood clubs and settings – wherever the quarrelsome rest their angry heads, confusion will follow. Strife, St. Thomas says, "gives rise to hatred and discord in the hearts of those guilty" of its commission.[32]

Sedition

Sedition represents the last in a series of offenses against the public order. Contrasted with strife, contention, and discord, sedition is a far more global offense against the common good. Sedition whips up and foments one group of people in antagonism to another. While not a war, the seditious man or woman incites and encourages others in a larger communal context to war upon one another. St. Thomas describes this practice as follows:

> Sedition, in its proper sense, is between mutually dissentient parts of one people, as when one part of the state

rises in tumult against another part. Wherefore, since sedition is opposed to a special kind of good, namely the unity and peace of a people, it is a special kind of sin.[33]

Sedition is the ultimate offense against the public order and public tranquility since it "involves a grievous offense against law and the common good."[34] Sedition foments uprisings, triggers civil disruption, and generates political chaos. Sedition "runs counter to the common good of the multitude"[35] and should always be construed as higher-level crime.

St. Thomas carefully distinguishes an uprising that challenges tyranny as being defensible to the charge of sedition. In fact, St. Thomas claims that the tyrant's very rule is inordinate and may in turn oblige the citizenry to rise up to overthrow the ruler.

> Indeed, it is the tyrant rather that is guilty of sedition, since he encourages discord and sedition among his subjects, that he may lord over them more securely; for this is tyranny, being conducive to the private good of the ruler, and to the injury of the multitude.[36]

With his usual deft practicality, St. Thomas gauges the defensible, non-seditious uprising in light of potential harms – as to whether maintenance of the tyranny might be less harmful than his overthrow. This tact edifies St. Thomas' radical theory of civil disobedience where moral agents are compelled to resist and not even recognize laws that are inconsistent with the eternal law. In the case of tyranny, St. Thomas calls for civil disobedience when "it is lawful to fight, provided it be for the common good."[37]

Public Indecency

Acts of indecency in the public realm will not be approved by St. Thomas primarily because these actions are intemperate. In the virtue theory of Aquinas, he, like Aristotle, continually searched for the mean and moderate of human behavior. Not that any type of conduct can be measured this way, for surely murder cannot be moderate nor child abuse. But in his larger, virtue framework, St. Thomas assesses a conduct's legitimacy according to its moderation. Public displays of sexual genitalia, for example, would leap off his virtue continuum. Public nakedness would fail similarly since the norm is to be clothed. Immodest clothing, cross-dressing, and other impropriety is condemned by Thomas. Add to this his view that a life of purity is to be favored over the decadent, and St. Thomas will frown on indecency in the public quarter. Display of anatomical body parts is both impure and unchaste and doing so should bring shame on the actor and consequence for its commission.[38] Public indecency brings not only shame but "certain disgrace" since the "vices of intemperance are especially disgraceful."[39]

St. Thomas urges all to live a life of purity and chastity – by reserving sexual conduct to the marital state. Any public exhibition would be contrary to this plan as Thomas argues: "For it belongs to chastity that a man makes moderate use of bodily members in accordance with the judgment of his reason and the choice of his will."[40] Thomas further supports his reasoning by reviewing the idea of modesty in outward movements. St. Thomas uses Augustine to make his point: "In all your movements, let nothing be done to offend the eye of another, but only that which is becoming to the holiness of your state."[41]

Modesty, aligned with temperance, deals with other actions that may prompt intemperance. To illustrate, immodest clothing may precipitate intemperate action. St. Thomas appreciates that some conducts precipitate or advance others. A lack of modesty, according to St. Thomas, may lead to intemperance. A wealth of modesty may preclude intemperance. More specifically, relevant to the law of crimes, modesty forbids public displays of indecency as they relate to "bodily movements and actions" which are unbecoming and dishonest, and those involving "outward show, for instance in dress and the like."[42]

From a contemporary perspective, St. Thomas may seem a lost cause. One need only gaze for a second at the current cultural landscape to conclude that it is over-sexualized, graphic to the point of pornographic, and by any measure reaching for the norm of immodesty in dress and behavior. In response to whether wives could adorn themselves within the confines of marriage, St. Thomas indicates that this is the proper place for the adornment. Searching for the mean and the moderate, St Thomas approves of the adornment when done "soberly and moderately" and not "excessively, shamelessly and immodestly."[43] On the other hand, outside this defined relationship, his approval vanishes.

> But to those women who have no husband nor wish to have one, or who are in a state of life inconsistent with marriage, cannot without sin desire to give lustful pleasure to those men who seem them, because this is to incite them to sin. And if indeed they adorn themselves with this intention of provoking others to lust, they sin mortally . . .[44]

St. Thomas shows little or no insight into how male indecency, particularly in the aggressive gay lifestyle, fosters immodesty with equal fervor. Uncomfortable St. Thomas would be in a world of pub and bar crawls, fellatio in parking lots, one night stands, triple "XXX" establishments and sexual prowling – the world being about as immodest as it is capable of being. A quick look at night spots, adult clubs, and entertainment for the singles' world would find infractions of every sort under his definition. Public indecency has gone mainstream in many circles.

In the final analysis, St. Thomas urges the human players to respect their personhood, their bodies and those they come in contact with. Outward movements and apparel should "be consistent with the estate of the person, according to general custom."[45]

Obscenity

St. Thomas writes only briefly about the tangible materials that portray pornographic content. The terms "obscenity" and "pornography" are outside his time and space. Even though depictions of sexual activity have been commonplace since early civilizations, the formal adjudication of these materials is a modern phenomenon. Obscene content is part and parcel of the indecency stream of thought in St. Thomas. At the end of his discussion on modesty in apparel, he raises the issue. "In the case of an art directed to the production of goods which men cannot use without sin, it follows that the workmen sin in making such things, as directly affording others an occasion for sin."[46]

Very similarly, the American test for obscenity weighs the illegitimacy of obscenity – discerning whether or not the materials have no purpose other than a prurient one. By prurient, the materials lack all scientific, educational, and artistic value and are produced exclusively to titillate and appeal to baser instincts. As Thomas indicates, the purpose for production is sin alone.

From a communal perspective, St. Thomas finds danger in the proliferation of this material, in much the same way that Plato did in his *Republic*. Art corrupts the masses if left unrestrained. St. Thomas would not be afraid to censor.

> In the case of an art that produces things which for the most part some people put to an evil use, although such arts are not unlawful in themselves, nevertheless, according to the teaching of Plato, they should be extirpated from the State by the governing authority.[47]

Hence both Plato and Thomas realize the negative and very harmful influences of public art that offends moral sensibilities. The current crop of television, theatre, and movie programming, to use St. Thomas' words, could only be described as "superfluous and fantastic."[48]

Summary

St. Thomas' stress on the common good and the collective naturally prompts concern about how individual citizens conduct their affairs. Individual behavior should always respect the rights of others. Aquinas treats offenses against the public order as if a mayor or a police chief would. He understands a great deal about human behavior – and especially how it impacts others. The chapter reviews public drunkenness, public disorder, discord, strife, and sedition. In the matter of drunkenness, St. Thomas posits a most curious theory on personal culpability and mitigation. It may be one of the few places where Aquinas shows excessive tolerance. In some cases, he simply exonerates the actor whose drinking squashed reason. His insights on those who sow discord in small as well as national circumstances are poignantly relevant.

Endnotes

1 St. Thomas Aquinas, *The Summa Theologica*, trans. Fathers of the English Dominican Province (New York: Benziger Brothers, Inc., 1947), II-II, Q 150, art 1 at 1799.

2 Glenn, *A Tour of the Summa* 278.
3 Aquinas, *Theologica*, II, Benziger, Q 150, art 1 at 1800.
4 Aquinas, *Theologica*, II, Benziger Q 150, art 3 at 1801.
5 Aquinas, *Theologica*, II, Benziger Q 150, art 3 at 1801.
6 Glenn at 278.
7 Aquinas, *Theologica*, II, Benziger Q 150, art 2 at 1800.
8 Aquinas, *Theologica*, II, Benziger Q 150, art 2 at 1800.
9 Aquinas, *Theologica*, II, Benziger Q 150, art 2 at 1801.
10 Aquinas, *Theologica*, II, Benziger Q 150, art 3 at 1801.
11 MPC § 4.01 et seq.
12 Aquinas, *Theologica*, II, Benziger Q 150, art 4 at 1802.
13 Aquinas, *Theologica*, II, Benziger Q 150, art 4 at 1802
14 Aquinas, *Theologica*, II, Benziger Q 34, art 3 at 1342.
15 Aquinas, *Theologica*, II, Benziger Q 34, art 4 at 1343.
16 Aquinas, *Theologica*, II, Benziger Q 34, art 6 at 1344.
17 Aquinas, Theologica, II, Benziger Q 37, art 1 at 1352.
18 Aquinas, *Theologica*, II, Benziger Q 37, art 2 at 1353.
19 Aquinas, *Theologica*, II, Benziger Q 37, art 2 at 1353
20 Glenn at 211.
21 Glenn at 211.
22 Aquinas, *Theologica*, II, Benziger Q 38, art 1 at 1354.
23 Aquinas, *Theologica*, II, Benziger Q 38, art 1 at 1354.
24 Aquinas, *Theologica*, II, Benziger Q 38, art 1 at 1354.
25 Aquinas, *Theologica*, II, Benziger Q 38, art 1 at 1354.
26 Aquinas, *Theologica*, II, Benziger Q 38, art 1 at 1354.
27 Aquinas, *Theologica*, II, Benziger Q 38, art 2 at 1355.
28 Aquinas, *Theologica*, II, Benziger Q 41, art 1 at 1363.
29 Aquinas, *Theologica*, II, Benziger Q 41, art 1 at 1363.
30 Aquinas, *Theologica*, II, Benziger Q 41, art 2 at 1364.
31 Aquinas, *Theologica*, II, Benziger Q 41, art 1 at 1363.
32 Aquinas, *Theologica*, II, Benziger Q 41, art 2 at 1364.
33 Aquinas, *Theologica*, II, Benziger Q 42,, art 1 at 1365.
34 Glenn at 213.
35 Aquinas, *Theologica*, II, Benziger Q 42, art 2 at 1366.
36 Aquinas, *Theologica*, II, Benziger Q 42, art 2 at 1366.
37 Aquinas, *Theologica*, II, Benziger Q 42, art 2 at 1366.
38 Aquinas, *Theologica*, II, Benziger Q 151, art 4 at 1804.
39 Aquinas, *Theologica*, II, Benziger Q 151, art 4 at 1804.
40 Aquinas, *Theologica*, II, Benziger Q 151, art 1 at 1802.
41 Aquinas, *Theologica*, II, Benziger Q 168, art 1 at 1877.
42 Aquinas, *Theologica*, II, Benziger Q 160, art 2 at 1847.
43 Aquinas, *Theologica*, II, Benziger Q 169, art 2 at 1883.

44 Aquinas, *Theologica*, II, Benziger Q 169, art 2 at 1883.
45 Aquinas, *Theologica*, II, Benziger Q 169, art 2 at 1883.
46 Aquinas, *Theologica*, II, Benziger Q 169, art 2 at 1884.
47 Aquinas, *Theologica*, II, Benziger Q 169, art 2 at 1884.
48 Aquinas, *Theologica*, II, Benziger Q 169, art 2 at 1884.

Chapter 8

Law, Justice, Sentencing, and Punishment

Introduction

A PENOLOGY WITH CONSEQUENCES APTLY DESCRIBES THE THOMISTIC IDEA of punishment. To restore equilibrium and balance caused by unjust activities, such as criminal behavior, St. Thomas legitimizes a penology of punishment. Punishment restores the imbalance in both temporal and eternal affairs. Punishment is what is due another. For most contemporary penologists, Thomas' methods of punishment seem out of the mainstream. Corporal punishment, dismemberment, and the death penalty are labeled acceptable reactions to injustice. Each of these practices either delivers a message of deterrence or removes a corrupted, infected member from the body politic. Thomas' insistence on restoration of the whole is quickly evident in his analysis of restitution, and he shows a keen awareness of victims' rights.

Punishment as Reciprocity

St. Thomas insists on corrective measures in any plan of systematic criminal justice. Despite the inherent goodness of the human species, admitting certain natural inclinations, and granting God's divine impression in creation, human beings still need correction and consequences in the event of doing wrong. Correction implies a soft or hard coercion and a series of guiding influences to keep the citizen morally erect. Punishment is "especially necessary against those who are prone to evil."[1] Rewards as well as punishments, Thomas indicates, are devised "so that men may be drawn away from evil things and toward good things."[2] Laws not backed by correction would be hollow admonitions. Laws, to be effective and binding, "must be obligatory, must have coercive power, and the coercive force of the law consists essentially in the fear of punishment."[3]

By their nature, corrective measures are consequences for activity injurious to both individual and society, and by its imposition seeks to correct an imbalance. Commutatively, punishment directs itself to a restoration of things and people, equalizing and correcting imbalances. In the legal system, punishment is commutative and corrective. Corrective justice is, by nature, a corrective measure, and a form of justice "which guides the judge not in determining whether a defendant has unjustly impinged in some way upon the interests of a plaintiff,"[4] but a response to a particular injustice.

Aside from this commutative quality, Thomas' theory of punishment, others assert, is grounded in its distributive counterpart [5] (allocating justice according to circumstance and individual characteristics). Thomas' depiction of legal justice deals with individual interrelationships and consequences in relation to others (*ad bonum alterius singularis personae*).[6] Punishment, therefore not only restores the equilibrium in a commutative sense, it assures or maintains the present order of economic, political, and social classes, and hence displays both commutative and distributive qualities.

In both civil and criminal cases, punishment and consequence seek to restore individual and community imbalance. Case by case, fact by fact, Thomas engages a penological theory of reaction to activity, and in a holistic sense where individual acts multiply to corrupt the common good. The entire justice system maintains its autonomy by meting out consequences, both individually and collectively.

Courtrooms are the perfect place to witness the experiment. The judge's very office expressly delineates "punishment" and other forms of correction as a judicial function. Punishment gives "the law its proper effect."[7] Thomas forcefully bolsters the legitimacy of judicial punishment in the *Summa Contra Gentiles*. "It is obvious that these men do not sin when they punish the wicked, for no one sins by working for justice. Now, it is just for the wicked to be punished, since by punishment the fault is restored to order, as is clear from our statements above. Therefore, judges do no wrong in punishing the wicked."[8]

Whether a criminal or civil case, harms to both person and state are injustices to be responded to. Silence and inactivity will not remedy the injustice. More particularly, judges cannot turn their heads or shy away from injustice. The task of the judge "is justice"[9] (*Judex dicitur quasi jus dicens*). If justice is rendering to each what is due,[10] justice's formula compels negative consequences. Those who do wrong are due something. Civilized societies and individuals attuned to virtue, the fundamental purposes of law and the importance of the common good, find corrective measures essential for its survival. Punishment is a form of lawful restraint, St. Thomas suggests, for its imposition restrains men from "wickedness," inducing them "to virtuous deed[s]."[11] Without punishment injustice would go unchecked and its effects multiply.[12]

Since justice is reciprocity and balance, those refusing its virtuous content, bypassing its virtuous instruction, snubbing its content, need suffer correctional consequences. Punishment is the *debt* that's due from one who owes another. Thomas terms debt a loss, a "detriment"[13] that needs elimination. In criminal cases, punishment responds to the sin of commission, Thomas concludes. Inherently, punishment is not wrong, but the inevitable by-product of wrongdoing. As such, punishment is "the effect of sin, not directly, but dispositively."[14] The debt of punishment only exists because of some malevolent act or disposition, some defect or excess of reason, or some "inordinate affection."[15] Punishment desires the settling of debts, the reestablishment of order, both to individual and community, and the quelling of chaos and disturbance. Thomas emphasizes its crucial role in legal or social systems. "As we have stated above, sin incurs a debt of punishment through disturbing an order. But the effect remains so long as the cause remains. Therefore, so long as the disturbance of the order remains, the debt of punishment must needs remain also."[16]

Punishment, even the severe variety, is legitimately inflicted for four reasons. First, punishment relates to the severity and gravity of the sin causing its imposition. A "greater sin, other things being equal, deserves a greater punishment."[17] Second, without punishment the human species would habituate to sin and misconduct and because of this negative reality, St. Thomas deems punishment a "cure" and a message for those who stray. Punishment serves a deterrent function also, both for the individual actor and those who learn from the punishment of others.

Allowing evil and error to go unchecked is a sure recipe for cultural disaster according to Thomas. Punishment is the bulwark fending off the madness in individual activity, and as an added benefit, it ensures tranquility and deters unacceptable behaviors. Punishment is inexorably tied to the *goods* integral to Thomistic thinking since a consequence is personal improvement.[18]

Communally, punishment screams its messages loud and clear. Thomas' visual imagery of the "hanged thief" is graphic and instructional. "Even the punishment that is inflicted according to human laws is not always intended as a remedy for the one who is punished, but sometimes only for others. Thus when a thief is hanged, this is not for his own amendment, but for the sake of others, who at least may be deterred from crime through fear of the punishment."[19]

Individually, punishment may sting enough, may prod enough to redirect, and even rehabilitate the individual offender. In teleological jurisprudence, the individual's goodness will surely lead to communitarian goodness. Punishment plays a significant role in the promotion of the common good. In select cases, punishment as disclosed by Thomas demonstrates a more global perspective than an unconditional concern for individual need. Human laws and their corresponding punishments sensibly include the following: "people are punished with death, not, of course, for their own improvement, but for that of others."[20] The reciprocal quality of punishment is one of Thomas' most attractive insights – as poignant today as in the time he uttered its content. A culture without consequence, without behavioral yardsticks, moral and legal standards and judgments, is ultimately short on justice.

Punishment, says St. Thomas, extends even beyond our temporal lifetime, as long as eternity. The "punishment of evildoers promotes the common good,"[21] and produces consequences that foster shared goals, stability, and general good (*bonum commune*) of the community.[22] Punishment in the right dosage can make men abhor wrong.[23]

God, according to St. Thomas, is both the ultimate lawgiver and issuer of just punishment.

In the *Summa Contra Gentiles*, punishment is always reserved for those erring, whence happiness is reserved for those living the good life. "Moreover, as good things are owed to those who act rightly, so bad things are due to those who act perversely. But those who act rightly, at the end intended by them, receive perfection and joy. So, on the contrary, this punishment is due to sinners, that from those things in which they set their end they receive affliction and injury."[24]

The legitimacy of punishment, in regards to the individual and the community, is not adjudged independently of its root philosophy. A corrupt philosophy is sure to foster a corrupt punishment ideology. Thomas' jurisprudence integrates his philosophical perspective into his penal justification. As such, punishment rectifies and repairs the injustice, promoting a reciprocity where all things are again in balance.

Types of Punishment and Penalties in Thomistic Jurisprudence

Thomas' analysis of punishment, its justification, type, and form, is an erudite penological theory, and includes: *relationship of punishment to offender, society and victim; a critique on the quality of criminal activity and criminal agency; theories of retribution; and, retaliation, vengeance, remediation and rehabilitation.* Thomas has unequivocal ends in mind, and his discussion of the diverse forms or types of punishment elucidate his correctional ideals.

Corporal Punishment

Contemporary perspectives on the role of corporal punishment are vastly different from those prevalent in Thomas' time. Modern thinkers, whether issuing opinions on child discipline, physical beatings in correctional facilities, whipping, flogging, and other physical assaults, even when emanating from proper authority, generally frown upon these practices. Invariably, these measures are labeled *cruel*, *unusual*, ruthlessly *unnecessary* and *barbaric*. To physically injure another, a behavioral scientist would argue, is to admit an inadequacy, not the inadequacy of the perpetrator of crime, but the inadequacy of the party charged with rehabilitation, especially in correctional facilities where the perpetrator resides. While remedial, resurrective change in the person is desirable, such optimism cannot preclude the application and imposition of physical force. Thomas even suggests that *maiming* is an acceptable reaction to criminality. Cutting off members of the human body – the legs, the arms, the hands, and so on – is both lawful and penologically sound. Thomas explains that dismemberment can be a wise application of judicial power, an exercise that Thomas reserves solely and exclusively to public authority:[25] "If, however, the member be decayed and therefore a source of corruption to the whole body then it is lawful with the consent of the owner of the member, to cut away the member for the welfare of the whole body, since each one is entrusted with the care of his own welfare."[26]

To illustrate, castration has, at times, been a punishment option in the Western, Eastern, and Islamic world. This cutting away of the sexual organ, the physical removal of the member of the body, would readily be lawful in a case of rape, pedophila, incest, sodomy, or other brutal crime. Without the sexual organ, the perpetrator will not again perpetrate, and for St. Thomas, excision of the organ benefits the common good. Even though contrary to the natural order and function of the body, the excision in select cases "is nevertheless in keeping with natural reason in relation to the common good."[27]

Thomas confirms the suitability of physical, corporal punishment in his discussion of vengeance. Whether punishments are an acceptable expression of vengeance will depend upon the motives for the vengeance. If the vengeance is borne of hatred, it will be an illegitimate exercise. If borne for a concern for the common good, vengeance justifies punishments involving "bodily safety"[28] including the "loss of eye for eye whereby man forfeits his bodily safety."[29] Thomas' affirmation of physical, corporal punishment is further buttressed in his analysis of parents and children. Present theories of child-rearing suggest an aversion to the use of physical control as a disciplinary response. Popular media and psychological punditry has made the practice all but anathema. To St. Thomas, the power of the parent is equated with the lawfulness of the physical correction. Spare not the rod but do not inflict "blows on them without moderation."[30] Insensible, unwarranted, disproportionate physical correction is not tolerated by Thomas, but for the maintenance of household and the corrective training of children, physical correction is expected. This power dimension, the authoritative justification, unfortunately allows the master to physically correct the slave in Thomas' world too. But this anomaly of justice is not based on a racist ideology, or a eugenic theory of mastery, but one of political, militaristic, and social authority. In this fashion, the slave is childlike, not as an inferior being, but as subordinate to authority. Children need training while, as harsh as it sounds, slaves need control. In both cases, physical control is an option.

Extending these principles to a penal setting, and accepting the legitimacy of a judicial sentence that imposes a physical punishment in place of incarceration, is consistent with Thomas' theory of punishment.

Imprisonment

The penological theory of St. Thomas generously allows the penalty of incarceration. The body of literature he provides on this topic is meager, but rich in justification. In responding to the query, *Whether it is lawful to imprison a man?*, he raises the dichotomy of free will and incarceration. How could a free willing, freely moving human agent be confined in space and time? Isn't imprisonment "inconsistent with free will?"[31] In ideal terms, Thomas agrees with the inconsistency, but quickly talks of the criminal's activity extinguishing the claim of freedom. Once, he argues, the criminal perpetrates, any natural claims based on freedom are forfeited. "A man who abuses the power entrusted to him deserves to lose it, and therefore when a man by sinning abuses the free use of his members, he becomes a fitting matter for imprisonment."[32]

Forfeiture, that loss of claim or right, is at odds with present criminological thinking, replaced with the talk of prisoners' rights, the right of rehabilitation, and the proliferation of correctional and constitutional law protections. This state of affairs is markedly opposite Thomas' correctional philosophy. Prisons are good for two reasons: 1) individual punishment; and 2) precaution against evil.[33] Prison represents a twofold rationale for incarceration, namely *deterrence* and the *infliction of punishment*. Both objectives are compatible with Thomas' view on why incarceration can and is a sound penal practice. Imprisonment is another venue for paying one's debt. Public authority has every right to imprison, St. Thomas says, but it is to "be done according to the order of justice, either in punishment or as a measure of precaution against some evil."[34] Imprisonment, without fault or the existence of morally evil action, would be disproportionate and unjust. Culpability is a prerequisite to its legitimacy, and the severity of the criminal act is pertinent to its duration. Thomas persistently condemns the lawmaker, the judge, or other lawful authority who imposes unreasonable sentences or other penalties.[35] Penalties disproportionately imposed, including that of imprisonment, are unjust if unreasonably related to the common good, an excessive burden or beyond the power of the judge or lawmaker.[36]

Mandatory prison terms for driving under the influence and drug-possession cases, habitual-offender statutes, and the extraordinarily harsh terms of imprisonment for domestic violence would be disfavored by St. Thomas. The term of imprisonment must correlate to the severity of the act. Novel or faddish criminalities, and of recent note, hate crimes, tend to exaggerate their seriousness, and as a result, oversell the punishment. Proportionality, that union of act and reaction, is always relevant in a penal context.

No doubt, talk of prisons and incarceration would be unnecessary if man were always virtuous. Human kind is predictably frail, and the nation and state need a consequence which promotes order. Imprisonment is a justifiable and lawful act that achieves this aim.

The Death Penalty

The Thomist resolve in matching consequences with particular criminal acts is markedly evident in the examination of the death penalty. Thomas is an unreserved, unequivocal supporter of the death penalty in certain cases. His words and argument rarely manifest hesitation, and in fact, there is a sort of ardent, passionate conviction typically found in the office of the district attorney.[37] In his *Commentary on Aristotle's Nicomachean Ethics*, Thomas exhibits no trepidation in the infliction of severe punishments. "[T]he insubordinate and the degenerate are allotted physical punishments like beatings and other chastisements, censure and loss of

their possessions. However, the absolutely incurable are extermi-
nated – the bandit, for instance, is hanged."[38]

At the same time, he employs the language of a surgeon who
saves the whole body from the corruption of its infected members.[39]
The legitimacy of this form of punishment is grounded in both theology and jurisprudence. Justifying the death of sinners to the bet-
terment of the common good, Thomas proclaims "[w]hen, however, the good incur no danger, but rather are protected and saved by
the slaying of the wicked, then the latter may be lawfully put to
death."[40]

Sinners, criminals are injurious to the whole and an imperfection eating away at community and culture, distracting us in our
imperfect journey to the perfect God. The death penalty simply
"puts to death those who are dangerous to others."[41] Writing from
a medical slant, Thomas urges the cutting away of infected members, the removal of rotted appendages and diseased bodily components whose infectiousness is sure to spread among the remaining
healthy parts. Bad individuals infect the whole in a similar way. An
example of the Thomistic method is evident when he states, "For
this reason we observe that if the health of the whole body demands
the excision of a member, through its being decayed or infectious to
the other members, it will be both praiseworthy and advantageous
to have it cut away."[42]

To justify the infliction, Thomas argues that the common good
replaces the individual need for self-preservation, and even though
self-preservation is an inherent, natural-law precept, *forfeiture* of
that right occurs by the conduct committed.

St. Thomas tempers this rigid approach by negating the possibility of the death penalty in a host of other circumstances. Clerics
and religious authorities are forbidden to kill the sinner/criminal,
for it is not within their competence to deal with human justice,
only matters of the spiritual,[43] since clerics are unqualified "to med-
dle with minor matters"[44] (*quod minoribus se ingerant*).

Also instructive is Thomas' admonition that man should not be
executed by private individuals since the act of the death penalty is
one of public authority and public justice. The care of the common
good "is entrusted to persons of rank having public authority."[45]
Only public officers may slay legitimately. The power of punishment

belongs to those in whose "office it is to impose the law; indeed, lawmakers enforce observance of the law by means of rewards and punishments."[46]

Mitigation, defensible conduct, and exculpatory rationales should not be disregarded when weighing the suitability of the death penalty.[47] Thomas' keen understanding of intentionality – the *mens rea* of a – criminal act is evident in his analysis of proportionate punishments. Chance events, accidents, negligent acts, or carelessness that causes the death of another mitigates the necessary level of intent to justify the death penalty.[48] Voluntary, willful acts incur the severity of death, and "chance happenings, strictly speaking, are neither intended nor voluntary. And since every sin is voluntary, according to Augustine (*De Vera Relig.* xiv) it follows that chance happenings, as such, are not sins."[49]

While a staunch supporter of the death penalty, Thomas passionately denies its applicability in cases of innocence, doubtful facts or insubstantial criminality. Levels of criminal victimization instruct the sentencing authority on the suitability of this extreme punishment. Thomas never ceases discussing the equitable quality of justice since the judgment of the death penalty should be "in accordance with the conditions of commutative justice, in so far as rewards are apportioned to merits, and punishments to sins."[50] In cases of innocent defendants, Thomas tolerates no death-penalty application. Not even the fact that the whole society can benefit from the loss of one innocent being, as a sort of constructive message, impresses Thomas. Death-penalty imposition is exclusively reserved for the culpable. The death of an *innocent* and just person is a gross injustice. The death of any just man robs the community of a meaningful member, but the execution of the unjust man, who "despises God more"[51] (*quia magis Deum contemnit*), aids communal tranquility. Thomas reserves acrid criticism for the judge who allows the innocent man to perish. "If the judge knows that a man who has been convicted by false witnesses, is innocent he must, like Daniel, examine the witnesses with great care, so as to find a motive for acquitting the innocent: but if he cannot do this he should remit him for judgment by a higher tribunal."[52]

If the evidence supports the death-penalty conclusion, the judge, even though he or she may personally believe otherwise, lacks discretion to alter the sentence because it is not "he that puts the innocent man to death, but they who stated him to be guilty."[53] The lack of hesitancy in Thomas to enforce and impose death-penalty punishments does not imply a cavalier attitude toward its severity nor a lack of deliberation on its applicability to varied circumstances. Few thinkers in history have so precisely forged and formulated a basis for its legitimacy. At its heart, Thomas determines that freely choosing beings socially exist with others, in communal settings, impacting one another whether conscious of it or not.[54] Just as telling is our own character, that which constitutes our good or evil character, either living in accordance with the law or not. For those who choose to undermine and undercut the collective whole, to infect, to riddle it with disease, there is a penalty of both punishment and forfeiture.

Those deliberating, choosing a life of criminality, lose more than the freedom of movement, the freedom of life as usually understood – they lose their essential dignity, the fundamental attributes that compose and construct the human species. Criminals forfeit rights not only because of their deeds, but because their deeds transform them into beasts.[55] By departing from the order of reason, man, says St. Thomas, falls "away from the dignity of his manhood, in so far as he is naturally free, and exists for himself, and he falls into the slavish state of the beasts, by being disposed of according as he is useful to others. . . . For a bad man is worse than a beast, and is more harmful, as the Philosopher states (*Polit.* i.1 and *Ethic.* vii.6)."[56]

In correctional parlance, one often hears the prison rank and file speak of the prisoners being "animals," acting like "apes," and having no sense of humanity. The registry of criminal deeds committed by the prison populace more often describes beasts rather than men.

Restitution

Another facet of Thomas' punishment/sentencing continuum is impressively ahead of its time – restitution. So often criminals serve time and incur punishments, but never make recompense to the victim. Victims are a necessary component in Thomistic criminal process. In restitution, the perpetrator is ordered to make the victim whole by paying for losses, compensating for damages, or returning what was larcened or converted. It is the quintessential act of commutative justice. Equilibrium is restored when property of equal or identical value is returned,[57] when payment for limb or loss of function compensates, when correction of a defamation or slander to name is publicized.[58] It is a wonderfully rich conception of making whole, of causing a restoration, or re-establishing equality from inequality.[59] In the criminal court, the judge has the power to effect restitution by a wide array of means. Restitution re-establishes equality since in every criminal case, the perpetrator is obliged to "restore just so much as he has belonging to another"[60] (*ad quod sufficit quod restituat tantum quantum habuerit de alieno*).

State after state legislature[61] has enacted *victims' compensation programs* which promote restitution in a manner that would cause joy for Thomas. Forcefully, Thomas forbids the criminal actor to be unaccountable, to hide behind mechanical, judicial processes that isolate victims of crime from the criminal's accountability. In Thomas' eyes, the victim deserves an apology by either word or deed, by compensation or substitute, and most importantly, by a system's effort to recast a loss in the closest, most complete sense. Victims are always, perennially, owed this debt, this restitution, even for eternity. Thomas could not be clearer when he comments that "He that has sinned is bound to satisfaction. Now restitution belongs to satisfaction. Therefore he that has taken a thing is bound to restore it."[62]

Putting off, excusing or delaying restitution is frowned upon too. To delay is merely to compound the sin already committed.[63]

Punishment and Salvation

Thomas blends, in a theological flavor, punishment, forgiveness, recompense, and salvation. A spiritual balance must be rectified – for those in sin, those who need to right their own injustices, are in need of a mechanism to correct personal harm or injustice. Punishment lends itself well to the restoration of this rectification. In general, punishment expresses a contrition of the soul, while the punished party simultaneously serves out the terms and conditions of the confinement. Every punishment ties itself to the spiritual health of the soul – an opportunity to repent and begin anew. It is a chance to live like the rational man God intended in his exemplar, to cast aside the slavish, brutish habits that dominate both intellect and will. If not, the eternity of the afterlife will not be in the ultimate end the joy and wonder of the Beatific Vision of God, but the misery and agony of damnation. St. Thomas is forever vigilant about the state of the perpetrator's soul. In response to whether mortal sin punishes forever, Thomas states that "he who is punished by this punishment, so that he is deprived of the ultimate end, must remain deprived of it throughout eternity."[64] Here is where Thomas' teleology gives brilliance to his criminology. Salvation should be the ultimate end of any penology. The penology proposed by St. Thomas doesn't debate the varied inherencies in the human condition, but is more than willing to perceive the human being as malleable, correctable, and changeable. The richness of St. Thomas' thought leads not to an intractable portrait of man, but one most capable of alteration and reform. It is optimistic because it believes in the power of reason and will, the strength derived from freedom itself. Any system of rewards and punishments cannot conclude otherwise. Thomas' penology ends its journey with the reminder that the most tragic of punishments is a lost felicity, the hopeless deprivation that comes from estrangement from God. The criminal's most pressing loss is in being "cut off from happiness."[65] The assurance of salvation is the ultimate aim of restitution and any other method of punishment.[66]

Summary

The correctional penology of St. Thomas rounds out the discussion of the Thomistic Crimes Code. If we accept that Thomas holds the free being accountable and culpable under most circumstances, and if we acknowledge that the free being inherently understands good and bad and is fully impressed with fundamental principles of the natural law, Thomas' penology will not be one without consequence. Surely consequence drives the correctional ideology, as if an Aristotelian who seeks restoration of the equilibrium and a return to things as they were previous to the criminal event. St. Thomas displays no hesitancy in meting out punishment. St. Thomas, at times, sounds even somewhat brutal. He never retreats from the right of public officials to execute, or these same players to hack off appendages, or doubt the propriety of imprisonment. This

is   a
correctional philosophy of cause and effect, consequence and result.
In the end, the restoration of the equilibrium must occur for the victim of crime, and for the community where the crime takes place,
but even more critically in the mind and soul of the perpetrator
whose salvation will remain in question.

Endnotes

1. Thomas Aquinas, *Summa Theologica, Basic Writings of Saint Thomas Aquinas*, Anton C. Pegis, ed. vol. 2 (New York: Random House, 1945), I-II, Q 100, art. 7, ad. 4.

2. Thomas Aquinas, *Summa Contra Gentiles*, trans. Vernon J. Bourke, vol. 4 (Notre Dame: University of Notre Dame Press, 1975) Book III, Part II, ch. 142, 3.

3. George Quentin Friel, "Punishment in the Philosophy of Saint Thomas Aquinas and Among Some Primitive Peoples," diss., Catholic University of America, 1939 (Washington, D.C.: The Catholic University of America Press, 1939), 123.

4. See W. J. Waluchow, "Professor Weinrib on Corrective Justice," *Justice, Law and Method in Plato and Aristotle*, ed. Spiro Panagiotou, (Alberta: Academic Printing & Publishing, 1987), 155.

5. For an insightful examination see Vernon Bourke, "Justice as Equitable Reciprocity: Aquinas Updated," 27 *The American Journal of Jurisprudence* 21 (1982): 21.

6. Bourke 19.

7. J. V. Dolan, "Natural Law and Judicial Function," *Laval Theologique et Philosophique*, 16 (1960): 107.

8. Aquinas, *Gentiles* III-II, ch. 146, 1.

9. Dolan 107.

10. St. Thomas Aquinas, *The Summa Theologica*, trans. Fathers of the English Dominican Province vol. II (New York: Benziger Brothers, Inc., 1947) II-II, Q. 58, art 11.

11. St. Thomas Aquinas, *On Kingsh*ip, trans. Gerald B. Phelan (Toronto: Pontifical Institute of Mediaeval Studies, 1982), Book II, ch. IV (I, 15) 120.

12. Friel 125.

13. Aquinas, *Theologica*, Pegis I-II, Q. 87, art 1.

14 Aquinas, *Theologica*, Pegis I-II, Q. 87, art 1, ad 2.
15 Aquinas, *Theologica*, Pegis I-II, Q. 87, art 1, ad. 3.
16 Aquinas, *Theologica*, Pegis I-II, Q. 87, art 3, c.
17 Aquinas, *Theologica*, Pegis I-II, Q. 105, art 2, ad 9. *quia majori peccato, caeteris paribus, poena gravior debetur.*
18 Brian Calvert, "Aquinas on Punishment and the Death Penalty," 37 *The American Journal of Jurisprudence* 263 (1992).
19 Aquinas, *Theologica*, Pegis I-II, Q. 87, a. 3, ad 2.
20 Aquinas, *Gentiles* III-II, ch. 144, 11.
21 Calvert 268.
22 Vernon Bourke, "The Ethical Justification of Legal Punishment," 22 *The American Journal of Jurisprudence* 4 (1977).
23 Aquinas, *Theologica*, II, Benziger II-II, Q. 108, art 3.
24 Aquinas, *Gentiles*, III-II, ch. 145, 4.
25 Aquinas, *Theologica*, II, Benziger II-II, Q 65, art 1.
26 Aquinas, *Theologica*, II, Benziger II-II, Q 65, art 1, c.
27 Aquinas, *Theologica*, II, Benziger II-II, Q 65, art 1, ad 1.
28 Aquinas, *Theologica*, II, Benziger II-II, Q 108, art 3, c.
29 Aquinas, *Theologica*, II, Benziger II-II, Q 108, art 3, c.
30 Aquinas, *Theologica*, II, Benziger II-II, Q 65, art 2, ad. 1.
31 Aquinas, *Theologica*, II, Benziger II-II, Q 65, art 3, obj. 1.
32 Aquinas, *Theologica*, II, Benziger II-II, Q 65, art 3, ad 1.
33 Aquinas, *Theologica*, II, Benziger II-II, Q 65, art 3, c.
34 Aquinas, *Theologica*, II, Benziger II-II, Q 65, art 3, c
35 Aquinas, *Theologica*, Pegis I-II, Q 96, arts 3 & 4. *See* James Ross, "Justice is Reasonableness: Aquinas on Human Law and Morality" *Thomist* 58 (1974).
36 See Ross 100.
37 Aquinas, *Theologica*, II, Benziger II-II, Q 64, art 2.
38 St. Thomas Aquinas, *Commentary on the Nicomachean Ethics*, trans. C. I. Litzinger (Chicago: Henry Regnery Company, 1964; Notre Dame, Ind.: Dumb Ox Books, 1994), X. L.XIV:C 2151.
39 Aquinas, *Theologica*, II, Benziger II-II, Q 64, art 2, c.
40 Aquinas, *Theologica*, II, Benziger II-II, Q 64, art 2, ad 1.
41 Aquinas, *Theologica*, II, Benziger II-II, Q 64, art 2, ad. 2.
42 Aquinas, *Theologica*, II, Benziger II-II, Q 64, art 2, c
43 Aquinas, *Theologica*, II, Benziger II-II, Q 64, art 4.
44 Aquinas, *Theologica*, II, Benziger II-II, Q 64, art 4, ad 2.
45 Aquinas, *Theologica*, II, Benziger II-II, Q 64, art 3.
46 Aquinas, *Gentiles* III-II, Chap. 140, 2.
47 Aquinas, *Theologica*, II, Benziger II-II, Q 64, art 7.
48 Aquinas, *Theologica*, II, Benziger II-II, Q 64, art 8.

49 Aquinas, *Theologica*, II, Benziger II-II, Q 64, art 8, c
50 Aquinas, *Theologica*, II, Benziger II-II, Q 61, art 4, ad 1.
51 Aquinas, *Theologica*, II, Benziger II-II, Q 64, art 6, ad 2.
52 Aquinas, *Theologica*, II, Benziger II-II, Q 64, art 6, ad 3
53 Aquinas, *Theologica*, II, Benziger II-II, Q 64, art 6, ad 3.
54 Calvert 277.
55 Aquinas, *Theologica*, II, Benziger II-II, Q 64, art 2, ad. 3.
56 Aquinas, *Theologica*, II, Benziger II-II, Q 64, art 2, ad 3
57 Aquinas, *Theologica*, II, Benziger II-II, Q 62, art 2, c.
58 Aquinas, *Theologica*, II, Benziger II-II, Q 62, art 2, ad. 2.
59 Aquinas, *Theologica*, II, Benziger II-II, Q 62, art 3, c.
60 Aquinas, *Theologica*, II, Benziger II-II, Q 62, art 3, c.
61 See Randy E. Barnett, "The Justice of Restitution," 25 *The American Journal of Jurisprudence* (1980).
62 Aquinas, *Theologica*, II, Benziger II-II, Q 62, art 6, sed contra.
63 Aquinas, *Theologica*, II, Benziger II-II, Q 62, art 8.
64 Aquinas, *Gentiles* III-II, ch. 144, 2.
65 Aquinas, *Gentiles* III-II, ch. 141, 3.
66 Aquinas, *Theologica*, II, Benziger II-II, Q 62, art 2, c.

Index

About the Author

CHARLES P. NEMETH, PROFESSOR, DIRECTOR OF GRADUATE LEGAL Studies and California University of Pennsylvania's Institute for Law and Public Policy, has spent his professional life engaged in the study of jurisprudence, the correlation of morality to law, ethics, and the relevance of classical and medieval thought in contemporary legal and judicial practice. A recognized expert on morality and legal ethics, appellate legal practice and private-sector justice, he is a prolific writer, having published numerous texts and articles on law and justice throughout his impressive career. His well-regarded, *Aquinas in the Courtroom* (Greenwood and Praeger Press 2001) is considered a work of immense originality since it prompts readers to find the Thomistic ethic as a recipe for justice. Other recent works include: *Private Sector Justice* (Prentice Hall, 2005), *Criminal Law* (Prentice Hall, 2003), *Law & Evidence: A Primer for Criminal Justice, Criminology, Law, and Legal Studies* (Prentice Hall, 2001) and *Private Security and the Law* (Elsevier, 2005). The bevy of peer reviewed publications manifest this unquenchable thirst for examining modern moral, ethical and legal dilemmas in law in light of perennial philosophical truths, as espoused by Augustine, Aquinas, and others. Works include commentaries on the role of judges and lawyers in Thomistic thought, the efficacy and morality of hiring quotas, the invasiveness of polygraphs, the decriminalization of child sexual offenses and a critique of good and evil in sociological and criminological circles.

Dr. Nemeth also serves the university as Director of the Institute of Law and Public Policy – a think-tank that sponsors regional and national forums, a university press, a myriad of publications and continuing education activities for the university and surrounding community. Subjects covered in the Institute's publications include the role of religion in judicial reasoning, a critique of precedent in the United States Supreme Court's overturn of criminalized sodomy, and the tension between terrorism and privacy.